D1097426

THIRD EDITION

CALGARY PUBLIC LIBRARY

MAY   2015

BEING CANADIAN

THIRD EDITION

Judy Cameron
Tracey Derwing

PEARSON
Longman

ERPI publishes and distributes PEARSON ELT products in Canada.
1611 Crémazie Boulevard East, 10th Floor, Montréal, Québec H2M 2P2 CANADA
Telephone: **1 800 263-3678**   Fax: **1 866 334-0448**
infoesl@pearsonerpi.com   **pearsonelt.ca**

Project Editor
Linda Barton

Art Director
Hélène Cousineau

Graphic Design Coordinator
Karole Bourgon

Cover Design
Benoît Pitre

Page Design and Layout
Fenêtre sur cour

© 2010 Published and distributed by

ÉDITIONS DU RENOUVEAU PÉDAGOGIQUE INC.

All rights reserved

 This book is explicitly excluded from any photocopy agreements in existence. Photocopying of any part of *Being Canadian* is illegal without prior written permission from the publisher.

Registration of copyright: 3rd quarter 2010
Bibliothèque nationale du Québec
National Library of Canada

Printed in Canada
ISBN 978-2-7613-3550-8
34567890 IG   18 17 16 15
 133550   ABCD   ENV94

RECYCLED
Paper made from
recycled material
FSC® C103567

This book is dedicated to our friend, Murray Munro
and to our partners, Scot Robertson and Bruce Derwing.

Preface

© PEARSON LONGMAN • REPRODUCTION PROHIBITED

Being Canadian, the third edition, is a reader suitable for students in LINC or other ESL programs where Canadian content is covered. The book is intended for students between Canadian Language Benchmarks 3 to 7. Using a topical approach, the text deals with the themes of social, cultural, and political history; physical and political geography; the structure of the parliamentary system and the electoral process; the nature of the economy; and globalization and the environment. In the third edition, all the chapters have been updated, new material has been added, and suggested grammar points for task-based focusing activities are provided at the beginning of each chapter. Many new activities are included, several of which involve the Internet. Websites containing relevant material are listed at the back of the book.

Being Canadian takes a content-based approach to learning ESL. The book focuses on contemporary Canadian issues as well as geography, history, government, and rights and responsibilities. The text shows the relationship among each of these areas, current situations, and the students' own lives. The contact activities in each chapter encourage students to apply their knowledge and skills outside the classroom, to become aware of and involved in community affairs, and to develop ties with people from a variety of cultural backgrounds. The materials in *Being Canadian* cover the issues and information contained in *Discover Canada,* the Citizenship and Immigration Canada guide for obtaining citizenship.

One unique feature of *Being Canadian* is its inclusion of sensitive issues and immigrants' viewpoints. The authors' own experience as ESL and citizenship instructors has made it clear that immigrants want to address both the positive and the negative aspects of an issue.

The chapters are designed as self-contained units; that is, it is not necessary to read them in any particular order. Furthermore, any chapter can be used as a supplement to other texts in ESL classrooms. Each chapter in *Being Canadian* contains realistic, captioned illustrations and photographs directly related to the text.

At the end of each chapter, there is a self-test section that allows students to test their knowledge of the material covered in the chapter. Answer keys are provided.

FORMAT OF THE BOOK

The book contains thirteen chapters that follow a similar format. Useful websites are listed in Appendix I. The general organization of each chapter is as follows:

Materials Required/Skills Emphasized

These sections tell the instructor what materials will be needed (for example, a map, a telephone directory) and which skills to emphasize (for example, reading, constructing a graph).

To the Teacher/Suggested Grammatical Focus Points

In these sections, suggestions are made for vocabulary and grammar points the teacher may want to emphasize.

Pre-readings

This section prepares students for the readings ahead. The pre-reading usually involves a graphic (charts, photos, flow diagrams, etc.) and accompanying questions (advanced organizers, general discussion questions, etc.).
This provides an opportunity for the teacher to determine the degree of knowledge that the students have and to build necessary vocabulary and concepts prior to doing the readings.

Readings

The readings provide a basic introduction to the topic.

Comprehension and Discussion Questions

This section presents comprehension questions that assess students' understanding of the reading, and discussion questions that draw from students' own experiences, backgrounds, and beliefs.

© PEARSON LONGMAN • REPRODUCTION PROHIBITED

© PEARSON LONGMAN • REPRODUCTION PROHIBITED

Language and Contact Activities

This section contains a variety of activities designed to reinforce the knowledge gained in the reading passage. It also develops language skills and encourages participation. Students are required to make lists, rank order items, describe, compare and contrast, make choices, evaluate ideas, develop generalizations, solve problems, read graphs, use the Internet, and so on. Contact exercises serve to engage students with their communities. For example, in Chapter 6, "Canada Today: A Diverse Society," students develop a survey of people's attitudes towards immigration. They interview people and then compile, analyze, and discuss their results.

Canadian Issues and Sidebars

Each chapter focuses on at least one interesting Canadian issue related to the main topic. Many of the issues give the instructor an opportunity to address sensitive topics. Most chapters contain one or more sidebars that provide interesting information related to the main topic.

Glossary

For each chapter, a glossary of new or difficult terms is provided. These terms are highlighted throughout the readings. A full glossary is included at the end of the book.

Test Yourself

Each chapter ends with test questions on the content covered in the unit. Answer keys are provided.

Teaching Tips

Each chapter includes a glossary of new vocabulary. Of course, there will be other words that students do not know. As they come across new or difficult words, ask the students to add the new words and their definitions to the vocabulary list at the back of each chapter.

Many students appreciate listening to the readings on their own. You may want to make digital recordings of the readings and send them electronically to students for home practice.

There are many resources available to teachers on the Internet (e.g., maps, quizzes, Canadiana pictures).

End-of-chapter reviews may be helpful for the students. Spelling bees, matching vocabulary with definitions, and content questions all help the students remember what they have learned.

Acknowledgements

We began teaching ESL classes over twenty years ago. Little did we know what a continuing impact our teaching experiences would have. Much of the material in this book stems from our own experiences and those of our colleagues and students. We are particularly grateful to Jeff Bullard, Patricia Dunne, Hilary Hellum, Jenny Maloney, and Wendy Rollins for the spirit of collaboration in which they shared their ideas. We would also like to acknowledge the National Working Group on Citizenship Education who contributed significantly to our view of participatory citizenship, the foundation of which is the mastery of an official language and knowledge about Canada.

There are many people who provided assistance in the development of this text. Several experienced ESL instructors read earlier versions and provided helpful suggestions for improvement. Liz Karra, Dean MacKay, Murray McMahon, Murray Munro, Albert Penner, Georgia Ramos, and Siegi Solti all gave useful input. A special thanks goes to Fiona Sime for piloting sections of the book in her ESL class. We would also like to thank Amber Gear, Marian Rossiter, Tara Holmes, and an anonymous reviewer for their assistance. As well, we appreciate the excellent suggestions and comments of Julie Hough, Vice President ESL (ERPI) and Linda Barton, Project Editor.

We would also like to thank NorQuest College, Edmonton for generously allowing us access to the college's LINC curriculum, and for giving us a chance to meet and interview ESL students. Thanks to Jerome Hendricks and other NorQuest staff for their openness. Finally, we acknowledge the incredible students we have met over the years. They continue to inspire us.

Table of Contents

© PEARSON LONGMAN • REPRODUCTION PROHIBITED

© PEARSON LONGMAN • REPRODUCTION PROHIBITED

© PEARSON LONGMAN • REPRODUCTION PROHIBITED

© PEARSON LONGMAN • REPRODUCTION PROHIBITED

© PEARSON LONGMAN • REPRODUCTION PROHIBITED

Chapter 1

What Does Canada Look Like?

MATERIALS REQUIRED: A large world map, a large map of Canada, a map of your province or territory, an atlas, several maps of your city, and pictures from various regions of Canada to supplement the readings. In addition, students should bring photos of their native country and currency from their country.

SKILLS EMPHASIZED: Reading comprehension, discussion, conducting a survey, expressing an opinion, making choices, comparing, identifying, classifying, describing, map reading, letter writing, listening.

TO THE TEACHER: Check the website list at the back of the book for relevant sites (e.g., Government of Canada, blank maps). Review vocabulary for seasons and weather. If your classroom has access to computers, ensure that Google Earth and Google Maps are installed.

SUGGESTED GRAMMATICAL FOCUS POINTS:

Reading I: prepositional phrases (e.g., *in the north, in central parts, on three sides*), comparatives and superlatives, *Wh-* questions, and definite articles.

Reading II: prepositional phrases (e.g., *through the prairies*), adjectives (e.g., *beautiful red sand beaches, wide open spaces, huge blue sky*).

PRE-READING I

- How many people do you think live in Canada?

- How many provinces are there in Canada?

© PEARSON LONGMAN • REPRODUCTION PROHIBITED

• What is a capital city?

• Can you name some oceans?

• What oceans surround Canada?

• How far do you live from the U.S. border?

• The **abbreviation** for the province of British Columbia is BC.
Do you know what an abbreviation is?

READING I
Canada

1   Canada is the second-largest country in the world (about 10 million square
kilometres) but it has a very small **population**. There are only about 33 million
people in the whole country. Most people live in the south and central parts
of Canada. Very few people live in the north. In fact, 75 percent (75%)
5 of Canadians live within 160 kilometres of the Canada-United States (U.S.)
border. Canada has oceans on three sides: the Pacific in the west, the Atlantic
in the east, and the Arctic in the north.

2   Canada is made up of ten provinces and three territories. The capital of
Canada is Ottawa, Ontario. The Canadian (federal) government is there.
10 Each province and territory also has a capital city. The provincial
governments are in the capital cities.

Provinces, Territories, and Capital Cities

PROVINCE/TERRITORY	ABBREVIATION	CAPITAL CITY
British Columbia	BC	Victoria
Alberta	AB	Edmonton
Saskatchewan	SK	Regina
Manitoba	MB	Winnipeg
Ontario	ON	Toronto
Quebec	QC	Quebec City
New Brunswick	NB	Fredericton
Nova Scotia	NS	Halifax
Prince Edward Island	PEI	Charlottetown
Newfoundland and Labrador	NL	St. John's
Northwest Territories	NT	Yellowknife
Yukon	YK	Whitehorse
Nunavut	NU	Iqaluit

© PEARSON LONGMAN • REPRODUCTION PROHIBITED

Map of Canada

© PEARSON LONGMAN • REPRODUCTION PROHIBITED

COMPREHENSION AND DISCUSSION QUESTIONS

1. Canada is the second-largest country in the world. What is the largest country? (Is it Russia, the United States, or Australia?)

2. What is the population of Canada?

3. What is the population of the country you come from?

4. Where do most Canadians live?

5. What countries or oceans are on Canada's borders?

6. What city is the capital of Canada?

7. What city is the capital of your country?

8. Which province do you live in? What is its capital?

LANGUAGE AND CONTACT ACTIVITIES

1. Map Reading and Cloze Exercise

Using a map of Canada or Google Earth, locate the following:

• the ten provinces and the three territories

• the capital of each province

• the capital cities of the territories

• the capital of Canada

• the largest province

• the smallest province

• the three oceans

• Hudson Bay

Fill in the blanks in the following paragraph. The first one has been done for you.

• Ottawa is the _____ *capital* _____ city of Canada. It is located in the province of

_____ *Ontario* _____, which is the largest province in Canada. The capital of the smallest

province, _____ is _____. The _____

Ocean is on west coast of Canada, bordering the province of _____.

The Arctic Ocean is in the _____ and the _____ is a large

body of water that touches Nunavut, Manitoba, and Ontario.

© PEARSON LONGMAN • REPRODUCTION PROHIBITED

2. Comparing Canada to Your Country of Origin

In groups, answer the following questions:

• Which country is larger, Canada or your first country?

• Which country has a larger population, Canada or your first country?

• Which is the largest city in your first country?

• What type of government is in power in the country you come from?

• Is the town or city where you live now larger or smaller than where you lived in your first country?

• What languages are spoken in your first country?

3. Your Journey to Canada

Interview a partner by asking the following questions. Write a paragraph about your partner's journey to Canada. The teacher will read the paragraphs aloud. Guess who the paragraph is about.

• What country are you from?

• What city or town are you from?

• When did you come to Canada?

• How did you get here?

• Where did you go first?

• Then where did you go?

• How did you feel when you arrived in Canada?

• Did you come alone?

• Why did you come to Canada?

• What did you know about Canada before you came here?

• What surprised you most about Canada?

4. Facts About Canada and Your Country

• Show your classmates some money from your country. What is the value of your **currency** in Canadian money?

• Put photos of your country around the room. Once all the students have put up pictures, guess which country each of the photos is from. Do any of the pictures look like places you have seen in Canada?

• Use an atlas and look up the size of your country of origin.

© PEARSON LONGMAN • REPRODUCTION PROHIBITED

On the chart below, fill in information about your country.

	CANADA	YOUR COUNTRY OF ORIGIN
Official languages	English and French	
Population	Small – 33,000,000 people	
Largest City	Toronto	
Government	Parliamentary **democracy**	
Currency	Canadian dollar	
Weather/Seasons	Hot in summer, cold in winter; 4 seasons	
Political Divisions	10 provinces and 3 territories	

PRE-READING II

In pairs:

• Locate the Trans-Canada Highway on the map of Canada.

• What cities are on the Trans-Canada Highway between Vancouver and Banff?

• Find the Great Lakes. What are their names?

• Find Thunder Bay and Sudbury in Ontario.

• Find Ottawa, Montreal, and Toronto. Find Moncton and Sydney.

• What city is directly north of Calgary?

• What city is directly south of Saskatoon?

• What city is northeast of Sydney, NS?

• Every map has a legend that tells you how to read the map. For example, most maps show how to measure the distance between two places. Using the map of Canada, find out how far it is between these cities:

Winnipeg to Regina	Toronto to Montreal
Calgary to Edmonton	Halifax to Fredericton
Ottawa to Montreal	Whitehorse to Yellowknife

READING II
A Trip Across Canada

1   The Trans-Canada Highway is the longest national road in the world (7821 kilometres). You can travel all the way from Victoria, British Columbia to St. John's, Newfoundland. Victoria, the capital of British Columbia, is on Vancouver Island. Victoria is one of the

© PEARSON LONGMAN • REPRODUCTION PROHIBITED

© PEARSON LONGMAN • REPRODUCTION PROHIBITED

warmest places in Canada—it
5 has mild winters and there are
flowers almost all year round.
To go from Victoria to
Vancouver, you take a **ferry**.
After a one-and-a-half-hour boat
10 ride, passing many small islands,
you arrive in Vancouver, the
third-largest Canadian city.
Vancouver is surrounded by
mountains and the Pacific
15 Ocean. Many people think it is
one of the most beautiful cities
in the world.

2 After driving all day through
mountains in British Columbia,
20 you will arrive in Banff, Alberta.
Banff is located in the heart of
the Rocky Mountains. **Tourism**
is the main business in Banff
and Jasper National Parks. In
25 the winter tourists ski, and in
the summer they camp and
hike. From Banff the Trans-
Canada Highway goes through
the **foothills** into the city of
30 Calgary. Calgary is famous for
its <u>rodeo</u>, the Calgary
Stampede.

3 After leaving Calgary, the
highway goes through the
35 **prairies** in Alberta,
Saskatchewan, and Manitoba.
After a day of driving through
wheat fields, you arrive in
Regina, the capital of
40 Saskatchewan. Another day on
the road brings you to
Winnipeg, Manitoba. Some
people don't like the prairies
because much of the land is
45 flat, but prairie people love the
wide open spaces and the huge
blue sky.

Victoria, BC is one of the warmest cities in Canada;
flowers bloom in Victoria all year round.

Dean Brandhagen

A winter scene of Banff in the Rocky Mountains

Canadian Tourism Commission/Commission canadienne du tourism

Visitors come from all over the world to see the rodeo
events at the Calgary Stampede.

Glenbow Archives NA-335-30

4   Just east of Winnipeg on the
     Trans-Canada Highway is a
50   **region** of rocks and trees.
     By the time you reach Ontario,
     the road starts to twist and turn
     for hundreds of kilometres.
     The first big city on the Trans-
55   Canada in Ontario is Thunder
     Bay. Thunder Bay is on Lake
     Superior, one of the five Great
     Lakes. The highway follows the
     lakeshore to Sault Ste. Marie
60   where Lake Huron meets Lake
     Superior. From there, the
     highway carries on to Sudbury,
     the nickel capital of Canada.

The Prairies

There are few trees around Sudbury; the earth is covered by rock. This area is part of
65   the geological region known as the Great Canadian Shield; nearly all of northern
     Ontario and Quebec are a part of the Shield. There is a lot of **mining** throughout the
     whole region, and some **forestry**, but very little farming.

5   The next large city on the Trans-Canada Highway is Ottawa, the capital of Canada. The
     Ottawa River is the border between Ontario and Quebec. Visitors will see a lot of rich
70   farmland outside Ottawa on the way to Montreal. Montreal is the second-largest city in
     Canada; it is also the second-largest French-speaking city in the world (Paris is the
     largest). Quebec City, the oldest city in Canada, is a three-hour drive from Montreal on
     the Trans-Canada Highway.

6   From Quebec City, the highway goes along the St. Lawrence River, then turns south
75   toward New Brunswick. New Brunswick is one of the four Atlantic provinces. New
     Brunswick is covered by green
     forests. Just east of Moncton,
     the Trans-Canada Highway
     forks in two directions. You
80   can go to Prince Edward Island
     (PEI) by the Confederation
     Bridge or by ferry or carry on
     to Nova Scotia. Prince Edward
     Island is the smallest province
85   and known for its beautiful red
     sand beaches.

7   Nova Scotians are never far
     from water or trees—this small
     province is almost completely
90   surrounded by the Atlantic
     Ocean and is covered with

Countryside in Quebec

© PEARSON LONGMAN • REPRODUCTION PROHIBITED

Provincial Archives of Alberta, Photo B2349

Canadian Tourism Commission/Commission canadienne du tourisme

forests. At Sydney, the northern tip of the
province, you can take a ferry to Newfoundland
and drive across the island on the Trans-
95 Canada Highway. Newfoundland is a rugged,
rocky island. Most of the people there come
from families who have fished the waters for
over a hundred years. Now, however, there are
very few fish left and many Newfoundlanders
100 are struggling to make a living.

Prince Edward Island is Canada's smallest
province.

Nova Scotia is famous for its maritime scenes.

Toronto is Canada's largest city.

8 Although the Trans-Canada Highway crosses
the southern part of Canada, it does not go to
some of the more important cities, including
Toronto (Canada's largest city), Edmonton, and
105 Halifax. However, there are major roads that
connect the highway to these cities.

Newfoundland and Labrador is Canada's most
remote province, located off the Atlantic shore
of the mainland.

© PEARSON LONGMAN • REPRODUCTION PROHIBITED

9 The largest region of Canada, the North, cannot be reached on the Trans-Canada Highway. Most
110 travelers go to the North by plane, although there are roads to Yellowknife, Whitehorse, and Inuvik. The North is a huge area where very few people live.
115 Much of the ground in the far North is frozen all year round. The North is divided into three Territories–Yukon, the Northwest Territories, and Nunavut.

Baffin Island is in the north of Canada, and is home to many Native people.

COMPREHENSION AND DISCUSSION QUESTIONS

• How do you get from Victoria to Vancouver?

• Why do tourists visit Banff and Jasper?

• Which provinces make up the prairies?

• What are the territories?

• Is the land good for farming around Sudbury? Why or why not?

• Which provinces in Canada have you visited?

• Which cities have you visited?

• Do you have friends or family who live in other provinces? Where do they live? How often do you see them?

• Where would you like to visit in Canada? Why?

• What is the farthest north you have ever been in Canada?

LANGUAGE AND CONTACT ACTIVITIES

1. Canada's Regions

Canada is made up of five regions listed in the chart on page 11. From the reading, fill in information about the landscape of the different regions. The landscape of the West Coast has been done for you.

© PEARSON LONGMAN • REPRODUCTION PROHIBITED

© PEARSON LONGMAN • REPRODUCTION PROHIBITED

REGION	PROVINCE OR TERRITORY	LANDSCAPE
West Coast	British Columbia	Pacific Ocean Mountains Forests
The Prairies	Alberta Saskatchewan Manitoba	
Central Canada	Ontario Quebec	
Atlantic Provinces	New Brunswick Nova Scotia Prince Edward Island Newfoundland and Labrador	
The North	Yukon Northwest Territories Nunavut	

2. Canadian Vacations

Choose a place in Canada that you would like to visit. Find it on a map or Google Earth and write two paragraphs about why this is a good place for a vacation. Be sure to answer the following questions.

• What is the name of the place?

• Where is it?

• How will you get there?

• Which provinces and/or territories will you travel through or over to get there?

• Is it near a lake, river, or ocean? If yes, what is the name of the water?

• What is the land like? Is it near the mountains? The prairies?

• Who will go with you?

• When will you go?

• What will you do when you are there?

• How long will you stay?

3. Internet Activity:
Finding Information About Places in Canada

More and more Canadians use their computers to find information. Use the Internet to find information about Peggy's Cove, a popular vacation spot in Nova Scotia. Use the Provinces and Territories website listed in the back of this book to help you get to

Nova Scotia. Once you have found the Nova Scotia website, go to the link for the tourism website. Find information on the following:

• places to stay in Peggy's Cove, restaurants, and museums

For more information, you could fax or write a letter like the one below. You could also ask for information by e-mail at explore@gov.ns.ca.

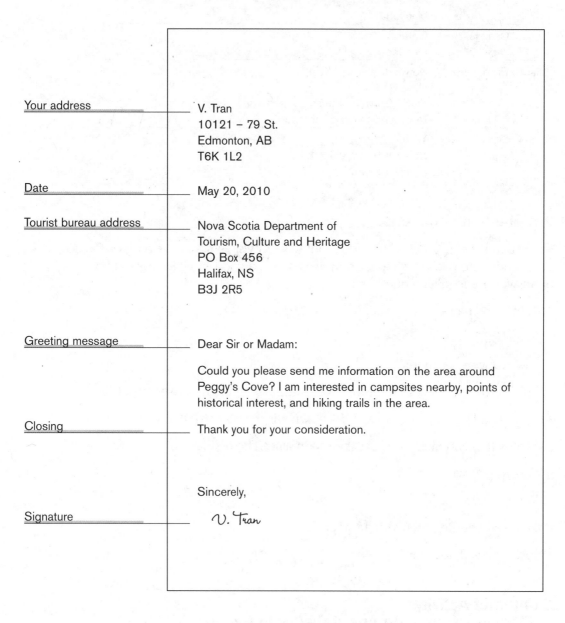

Your address

V. Tran
10121 – 79 St.
Edmonton, AB
T6K 1L2

Date

May 20, 2010

Tourist bureau address

Nova Scotia Department of
Tourism, Culture and Heritage
PO Box 456
Halifax, NS
B3J 2R5

Greeting message

Dear Sir or Madam:

Could you please send me information on the area around Peggy's Cove? I am interested in campsites nearby, points of historical interest, and hiking trails in the area.

Closing

Thank you for your consideration.

Sincerely,

Signature

V. Tran

© PEARSON LONGMAN • REPRODUCTION PROHIBITED

Now, choose a vacation spot where you would like to go. Using the Internet, find the address of the tourist bureau and write a letter requesting information about the place. Your letter should have all of these parts: your address, date, tourist bureau address, greeting message, closing, and signature.

© PEARSON LONGMAN • REPRODUCTION PROHIBITED

Canadian Issue

Weather and Climate

Canadians like to talk about the weather. The weather can change very quickly. The **chinooks** of southern Alberta are a good example. Warm, dry winds blow over the Rocky Mountains and can raise the temperature in Calgary from −15°C to +10°C within a few hours.

The **climates** in Canada's five regions are all different. On a winter day, the temperature in Victoria may be +10°C while in Whitehorse and Montreal, it may be −30°C. Canadians enjoy long hours of sunlight in the summer; many people play sports or just sit outside until late into the evening. In the winter, people are used to very short days and long nights. In northern towns such as Inuvik, the sun doesn't rise at all in the middle of the winter. The North is called the Land of the Midnight Sun in the summer because people can enjoy up to 24 hours of daylight.

Driving in the winter can be a challenge.

Provincial Archives of Alberta, Photo J3808/1

When people first come to Canada, they are often shocked by the weather. They know before they come that Canada has cold winters, but you have to live through a winter before you can really understand why people plug in their cars, wear several layers of clothes, and use a lot of energy to heat their houses.

Follow-up

• When Canadians talk to strangers, they often talk about the weather. It is the easiest way to start a conversation. What do strangers talk about in your first country?

• In your community, how many ways are there to find out what the weather **forecast** is for tomorrow?

• Listen to the news on the radio or TV. Find out what the weather forecast is for tomorrow.

• What's the coldest temperature you have ever experienced? The hottest?

GLOSSARY OF TERMS

NOUNS

abbreviation
a short way to write a word

border
invisible line separating two
countries or provinces

chinook
dry warm wind

climate
a combination of temperature,
precipitation (rain or snow), wind, etc.

currency
money

democracy
a government that is elected by the
people, and that can be changed by
the people

ferry
a boat that takes cars and/or people
across water

foothills
large hills close to mountains

forecast
weather prediction

forestry
the industry of cutting trees and turning
them into lumber and paper

mining
taking minerals such as gold or iron
from the earth

population
total number of people in a place

prairie
flat, dry land

region
area, place

rodeo
a competition in which cowboys ride
wild horses, rope cattle, and perform
in other events

tourism
hotels, restaurants, sightseeing tours, travel

VERBS

to connect
join

Test Yourself

What Does Canada Look Like?

MULTIPLE CHOICE

Circle the best answer.

1. Canada is the _____ country in the world.

   A) largest   C) third-largest

   B) second-largest   D) fourth-largest

2. Canada has _____ official language(s).

   A) one   C) three

   B) two   D) more than three

© PEARSON LONGMAN • REPRODUCTION PROHIBITED

3. Canada has _____.
   A) eight provinces   C) four territories
   B) ten provinces   D) one territory

4. Fredericton is the capital of _____.
   A) Nova Scotia   C) New Brunswick
   B) Prince Edward Island   D) Newfoundland and Labrador

5. The largest city in Canada is _____.
   A) Toronto   C) Montreal
   B) Ottawa   D) Vancouver

6. The capital of Canada is _____.
   A) Toronto   C) Montreal
   B) Ottawa   D) Vancouver

7. Canada is bordered by all but the _____ Ocean.
   A) Arctic   C) Atlantic
   B) Pacific   D) Indian

TRUE/FALSE

Circle *T* if the statement is true. Circle *F* if it is false.

1. Canada is made up of twelve provinces. T / F

2. The capital city of Canada is Ontario. T / F

3. The capital of British Columbia is Vancouver. T / F

4. The capital of Ontario is Montreal. T / F

5. Vancouver is the third-largest city in Canada. T / F

6. The population of Canada is approximately 33 million. T / F

7. Canada is surrounded by two oceans. T / F

8. Most Canadians live in the southern part of Canada. T / F

FILL IN THE BLANKS

In the blank space(s), write the word(s) needed to make the sentence complete.

1. The population of Canada is approximately _____ million.

2. _____ is the capital of Yukon.

3. The country to the south of Canada is _____.

4. _____ is the capital city of Saskatchewan.

5. St. John's is the capital city of _____.

6. The largest city in Canada is _____.

© PEARSON LONGMAN • REPRODUCTION PROHIBITED

7. The official languages of Canada are _____ and _____.

8. Canada is made up of _____ provinces and _____ territories.

9. The capital city of British Columbia is _____.

10. Canada is surrounded by the _____, _____, and _____ oceans.

MATCHING

Match each capital city with the province/territory it belongs to.

A. British Columbia	____	Yellowknife
B. Alberta	____	Fredericton
C. Saskatchewan	____	Edmonton
D. Manitoba	____	Charlottetown
E. Ontario	____	Whitehorse
F. Quebec	____	Toronto
G. New Brunswick	____	Iqaluit
H. Nova Scotia	____	Winnipeg
I. Prince Edward Island	____	Victoria
J. Newfoundland and Labrador	____	Halifax
K. Northwest Territories	____	Quebec City
L. Yukon	____	St. John's
M. Nunavut	____	Regina

SHORT ANSWER

Answer the following questions.

1. Which oceans surround Canada?

_____

2. List the Great Lakes.

_____

3. Name the prairie provinces.

_____

4. What is a chinook?

_____

5. What are the names of the territories in the north?

_____

6. Which are the four Atlantic provinces?

_____

© PEARSON LONGMAN • REPRODUCTION PROHIBITED

© PEARSON LONGMAN • REPRODUCTION PROHIBITED

Chapter 2

Canada's First Peoples

MATERIALS REQUIRED: Maps of Canada and the world, *The Canadian Encyclopedia,* and information and pictures related to Native peoples in your area.

SKILLS EMPHASIZED: Map-reading skills, letter writing, reading a timeline, discussing, planning, listing ideas, reading for information, explaining, expressing opinions.

TO THE TEACHER: Check the website www.aboriginalcanada.gc.ca for information about aboriginal peoples in Canada. Go over the format for writing letters, and discuss vocabulary related to hunting and fishing.

SUGGESTED GRAMMATICAL FOCUS POINTS:

Reading I: past tense, time expressions (e.g., *30 000 years ago*), relative clauses (e.g., *Native people who lived in eastern and central Canada were farmers*).

Reading II: exemplification (e.g., *such as, for example, including*).

PRE-READING I

Canada is made up of many different people.

PEOPLE	ARRIVAL	REASON FOR COMING TO CANADA
Indians (First Nations)	30 000 years ago	to hunt, farm, and fish
Inuit	5000 years ago	to hunt and fish
English	1497	to fish
French	1534	to hunt, farm, trade furs
Chinese	about 1870	to build the railroad
Other Europeans	1885-1910	to farm
People from elsewhere	present	for freedom, to start a new life

National Archives of Canada / C-011336

Indians living in British Columbia

- Have you ever heard of the Indian, Inuit, and Métis people?
- Who were the first people to come to Canada?
- How much longer have the Inuit been in Canada than the English?
- For what reasons do most people come to Canada now?
- When did you come to Canada? Why did you come to Canada?
- If you had to do it over, would you still come to Canada?

Here is a timeline. Above the timeline are dates. Below the timeline are events. Fill in the information from the chart on page 17.

30 000 years ago	5000 years ago	1497	1534	1885-1913	now

Indians arrive in Canada   My arrival in Canada

READING I
Indians, Inuit, and Métis

1 The first people to come to Canada were the Indians. Scientists think that they came from Asia across the Bering Strait about 30 000 years ago. When they arrived in North America they traveled south and east. After several hundred years there were many groups of **Native people**

5 who had different cultures and languages. There are more than fifty Indian languages in Canada. Today, North American Indians are often called First Nations Peoples.

2 10 The Indian people who lived by the coasts hunted and fished. Prairie Indians moved from place to place, hunting the **buffalo**. They ate buffalo meat and used buffalo

15 **hides** to make clothing and **teepees**. Some Native people who lived in central and eastern Canada were farmers. They grew corn and vegetables.

Glenbow Archives NA-1700-56

Totem poles in Alert Bay, British Columbia

© PEARSON LONGMAN • REPRODUCTION PROHIBITED

Huge herds of buffalo roamed the prairies before the arrival of the Europeans.

Glenbow Archives ND-8-247

A Native teepee

Richard Harrington / National Archives of Canada / C-024214

3 20 The **Inuit** (also called Eskimo) came to Canada from Asia about 5000 years ago. They moved across the north from Alaska to Greenland, and learned to live in a land of ice and snow. They lived by hunting
25 seals, whales, caribou, and polar bears. Many lived in ice houses called igloos. Today many Inuit still hunt. Most live in small towns in northern Canada.

Inuit hunter

Canadian Tourism Commission/Commission canadienne du tourisme

4 In the 1500s, people from Europe started
30 to come to Canada to live. Some Native people showed them how to **survive**. They helped them with food and shelter. They **guided explorers** to new lands and helped to **establish** the fur trade. Some Native people married Europeans. Their children were called Métis. The Métis people developed their own **culture** and
35 customs. The Indians, the Inuit, and the Métis are referred to as aboriginal peoples and are all citizens of Canada today.

Potlatches were celebrations at which groups of West Coast Indians feasted and exchanged gifts.

British Columbia Archives, Photo #E-04017

© PEARSON LONGMAN • REPRODUCTION PROHIBITED

Inuit mother and child

A group of Innu making canoes in Labrador.

COMPREHENSION AND DISCUSSION QUESTIONS

1. When did the Indian people come to Canada?

2. When did the Inuit come to Canada?

3. How did the Indian people survive?

4. Where do the Inuit live today?

5. What did you know about Canada's Native people before you came to Canada?

6. What do you know about the Native people in your community?

7. Are there any whales, seals, caribou, or bears in the country you came from?
   What animals live in the wild there?

LANGUAGE AND CONTACT ACTIVITIES

1. Map Reading: The World

With a partner, look at a map of the world. Locate Asia, North America, Canada, Alaska, and the Bering Strait. Mark the route the Native people took to come to Canada.
What kind of transportation do you think the Native people used to come to Canada?

© PEARSON LONGMAN • REPRODUCTION PROHIBITED

2. Map Reading: Canada

Inuit people still live in northern Canada. On a map of Canada, locate the Inuit communities of Inuvik, Iqaluit (Frobisher Bay), Arviat (Eskimo Point), Rankin Inlet, and Tuktoyaktuk. How far is each of these places from where you live? Which place is the closest? Which is the farthest?

3. Hunting and Fishing

Use your telephone directory or the Internet to find the government department in your province responsible for hunting and fishing licences. Answer the following questions.

• How much does a hunting licence cost?

• How much does a fishing licence cost?

• Where can you hunt?

• Where can you fish?

• Are there places where hunting and fishing are not allowed?

• What animals can be hunted?

Some people think of hunting as a sport. That is, they hunt for fun. Other people only hunt for food. Do you think hunting should be allowed as a sport?

PRE-READING II

• What do you think happened when the Europeans first met the Native people in Canada?

• Have you heard of smallpox, measles, tuberculosis? Were these **diseases** ever a problem in the country you came from?

• Do you know what an Indian **reserve** is?

READING II
Native Values

1 When the Europeans came to Canada, the life of the Native people changed forever. Europeans brought serious diseases such as smallpox, measles, and tuberculosis. Tens of thousands of Native people died.

2 When the Europeans started **colonies** in the Atlantic provinces and central Canada,
5 farming became important. Indians were **forced** off their lands and onto small reserves (land for Native use only). For many years, Native people have been unhappy with the way the Europeans treated them. They want agreements that will give them the land that they feel belongs to them.

© PEARSON LONGMAN • REPRODUCTION PROHIBITED

3
10 Losing people to disease and losing land to the Europeans were not the only problems faced by the Native people. From the mid-1800s to the mid-1990s, Native children were forced to leave their families and go to residential schools. The purpose of these schools was to **assimilate** Natives into European culture. Children were not allowed to speak their own language or practice their customs and they were often abused. In 2008, the Canadian government apologized for this practice.

4
15 Native people's **values** are very different from European values. The ideas of **cooperation**, sharing, and **respect** for the land are important to the Native peoples. Europeans value **individual achievement** and **private ownership**.

5
Today, Native people face many serious social problems including **discrimination**, poor education, **alcoholism**, and high unemployment. There are some people who have a
20 **stereotyped** idea about Native people. For example, they think that all Native people receive a living allowance from the government. In fact, many Native people do not receive a living allowance or any other government assistance. Native people in cities and on reserves are trying to get greater control over their lives; they want to solve their problems and many would like to have self-government.

COMPREHENSION AND DISCUSSION QUESTIONS

1. When the Europeans first came to Canada, they tried to force the Native people to adopt European culture. What were the effects?

2. Which values of the Native peoples and which values of the Europeans caused **conflicts**? Why?

3. Do you think that a person must give up his or her own culture in order to become a Canadian?

4. Native people experience a lot of discrimination. Why do you think this is? Have you experienced any discrimination as an immigrant? What can we do to stop discrimination?

5. How are Native and European values different?

6. Which do you think the Canadian government values more—individual rights or society's rights? Which do you think are more important?

LANGUAGE AND CONTACT ACTIVITIES

1. Invite a Guest Speaker to Class

Write a letter to your local Native Friendship Centre or Native Community Centre to invite a guest speaker to your class to talk about Native issues. Make up a list of questions to ask the guest speaker. A list has been started for you.

© PEARSON LONGMAN • REPRODUCTION PROHIBITED

• What languages do you speak?

• Are there many Native people in your city/town?

• What does the Native Friendship Centre do?

2. Plan a Field Trip to Your Local Museum

As a group, make up a list of questions to ask the museum guides. Here are some questions you might ask:

• Does the museum have a Native people's display?

• When is the museum open?

• How much does it cost?

Choose one student to phone the museum, find out the answers to the questions, arrange a date for the class to visit the museum, and report back to the rest of the class.

3. Newspaper Stories

Look through your local newspaper for one week. Find one article about Native people. Bring the article to class. In pairs, tell your partner about the article by answering the following questions:

• Who is the article about?

• What happened?

• Where did it happen?

• When did it happen?

4. Aboriginal Words

The word *Canada* comes from the aboriginal word *kanata,* meaning village. Many place names in Canada come from aboriginal languages, including *Saskatchewan, Ottawa,* and *Nunavut. Saskatchewan* comes from a Cree word meaning *swiftly flowing river. Ottawa* comes from the name of a tribe (it means *to trade*) and *Nunavut* means *our land.* Name three more places that come from aboriginal words and find their meanings in *The Canadian Encyclopedia* or on the Internet.

Canadian Issue

The Native Land Claims Issue

Once Europeans gained control of what is now Canada, they began to make land agreements with the Native people. That is, they offered to let the Native people keep small areas of land that would be for Native use only (reserves). Some Native groups received reserve land; others did not. Recently, several Native groups have argued that they should be given back the land that was taken away from them.

© PEARSON LONGMAN • REPRODUCTION PROHIBITED

The federal, provincial, and territorial governments are meeting with some Native groups. Some Native bands have been successful; the government has given them more land and/or money. Other Native bands, such as the Lubicon Indians in northern Alberta, are still fighting for their land.

Follow-up

• All of North America once belonged to the Native people. Do you think it is fair that the land was taken away from them? Do you think that the land that was taken away should be given back?

• Look up the Lubicon Indians in *The Canadian Encyclopedia* or on the "Friends of the Lubicon" website (http://tao.ca/~FOL/index.html). Try to answer the following questions:

– Who are the Lubicon Indians?

– Where do they live?

– When did they start to argue about land with the government?

– What happened?

GLOSSARY OF TERMS

NOUNS

achievement
success

alcoholism
addiction to alcohol

buffalo
a large animal that lived on the prairies

colonies
places to live set up by Europeans outside Europe

conflict
disagreement or argument

cooperation
working together

culture
the beliefs, values, and lifestyle of a group of people

discrimination
pre-judging on the basis of sex, skin colour, religion, etc.; prejudice

disease
sickness, illness (e.g., smallpox, flu, malaria, cholera, tuberculosis)

explorer
someone who travels to places that were previously unknown

hide
the skin of an animal

individual
one person

Inuit
aboriginal people who live in the north, also called Eskimo

Native people
aboriginal people, Indians, First Nations people

private ownership
things belong to individuals, not to the community

reserve
land owned by Native people

respect
appreciation, good treatment

stereotype
a standardized image or idea about a person or group of people

© PEARSON LONGMAN • REPRODUCTION PROHIBITED

teepee
a tent made of hides and wooden poles
values
what people believe in

VERBS

to assimilate
to absorb, to take in

to establish
to start, to set up
to force
to make someone do something
to guide
to show the way
to survive
to continue to live, to succeed

Test Yourself

Canada's First Peoples

MULTIPLE CHOICE

Circle the best answer.

1. Who were the first people to come to Canada?
   - A) the English
   - B) the French
   - C) the Indians
   - D) the Americans

2. How many Indian languages are there in Canada today?
   - A) less than 10
   - B) 10-20
   - C) 25-50
   - D) more than 50

3. People whose parents (or ancestors) are both Native and European are called _____.
   - A) Inuit
   - B) Métis
   - C) Inuvik
   - D) Mohawk

4. Indians came to Canada approximately _____ years ago.
   - A) 50 000
   - B) 30 000
   - C) 5000
   - D) 3000

5. An area of land that is set aside for use by Native people only is called _____.
   - A) a reserve
   - B) Indiana
   - C) an Indian band
   - D) a territory

TRUE/FALSE

Circle *T* if the statement is true. Circle *F* if it is false.

1. Europeans brought many diseases to the aboriginal peoples. T / F

2. The English were the first to come to Canada. T / F

3. All Native people speak the same language. T / F

© PEARSON LONGMAN • REPRODUCTION PROHIBITED

4. The Indian people helped the Europeans to survive. T / F

5. Métis are people whose ancestors were both Native and European. T / F

FILL IN THE BLANKS

In the blank, write the word(s) needed to make the sentence complete.

1. The Inuit lived in ice houses called _____.

2. The Indian people came to Canada approximately _____ years ago.

3. The Inuit came to Canada approximately _____ years ago.

4. The English first arrived in Canada in _____.

5. The French first settled in Canada in _____.

6. The Indian people living on the coasts survived by _____ and _____.

7. The Indian people living on the prairies survived by _____.

8. The Indian people living in central Canada survived by _____.

9. The Indian people were forced off their land and onto _____.

SHORT ANSWER

Answer the following questions.

1. How do scientists think Indian people came to Canada?

2. What happened to the Indian people when Europeans first came to Canada?

3. What is a reserve?

4. List two values of Native people.

5. List three problems that Native people face today.

© PEARSON LONGMAN • REPRODUCTION PROHIBITED

Chapter 3
Our English and French Heritage

© PEARSON LONGMAN • REPRODUCTION PROHIBITED

MATERIALS REQUIRED: Map of North America, pictures and other resources about early French and English settlers, *The Canadian Encyclopedia.*

SKILLS EMPHASIZED: Reading comprehension, discussion, expressing an opinion, comparing, listing, evaluating, describing, organizing information, predicting, listening, giving instructions.

TO THE TEACHER: Show students how to use a search engine (e.g., Google) to find information on the Web. The Historica-Dominion Institute website (listed at the back of this book) is a useful supplement to many of the activities in this chapter. Go over language for giving directions (e.g., *turn right, turn left, go straight ahead*) and terms for sequencing information *(first, next, and then).* Cover discourse markers useful for debates such as "on the contrary", "and another thing", "therefore", "consequently", and so on.

SUGGESTED GRAMMATICAL FOCUS POINTS:
Reading I and Reading II: passive voice (e.g., *was founded, was forced, is spoken, are found).*

PRE-READING I

• On a map of Canada, find Newfoundland and Labrador, Quebec City, and the St. Lawrence River.

• Are there very many French speakers in your community? Do you have a French TV station? Radio station?

• How did the first French and English people survive when they came to Canada?

READING I
The English and French Come to Canada

1   Although the Vikings (from Iceland) were the first Europeans to come to Canada, they did not stay permanently. In 1497 Giovanni Caboto (also known as John Cabot) sailed from England to Newfoundland. He claimed the land for the King of England. The English were glad that Caboto found Canada because the fishing was very good.
5   Every summer, many ships sailed to Newfoundland to fish off the Grand Banks and then would return to England for the winter.

2   In the early 1500s the French came to Canada. They were the first **permanent settlers** from Europe. They set up fur **trading posts** in Acadia (parts of Nova Scotia, New Brunswick, and Prince Edward Island) and along the St. Lawrence River. The first
10 Canadian city, Quebec City, was founded by Samuel de Champlain on the site of an older Indian village called Stadacona. The French lived by hunting, farming, and fur trading with the Indians (First Nations people). The First Nations people brought **pelts** of beaver and other animals to the French, who traded blankets and **trinkets** in return. The French then sold the pelts in Europe for a lot of money.

An Indian chief trading

3   15 The English began to **settle** in Canada too. There were many **struggles** between the French and the English for control of Canada. In 1759, in the Battle of the Plains of Abraham (outside Quebec City), British General James Wolfe and his troops defeated the French army led by General Montcalm. In 1763, at the end of the Seven Years' War (between England and France), France was forced to give all its land in North America to
20 England. The Canadian colonies now had an English king, but the **majority** of the people who lived there were French.

4   Although the colonies in what is now Quebec came under British control, the Quebec Act of 1774 gave the people in that region some basic rights (freedom of religion and

O.B. Buell / National Archives of Canada / PA-118768

© PEARSON LONGMAN • REPRODUCTION PROHIBITED

French civil law). The
25 British traveled to the West,
where they set up fur trading
posts and settlements.
Today, English is spoken
by the majority of people
30 in Canada. The Canadian
system of government
is based on the British
system.

5 About 80 percent of
35 the people living in
Quebec speak French
as a first language.
French speakers are
also found in every part of
40 Canada. There are French
newspapers, radio, and TV
stations across the country.

Trading furs for food supplies

COMPREHENSION AND DISCUSSION QUESTIONS

1. Why did the English come to Newfoundland every summer?

2. Who were the first European settlers in Canada?

3. What was the first city in Canada?

4. Which province has the most French-speaking people?

5. What did the English and French trade with the First Nations people?

6. Do you speak French?

LANGUAGE AND CONTACT ACTIVITIES

1. Finding Two Sides to an Issue

Fur has always been important in Canada's history. Today there are people called animal rights activists who are against the killing of animals for any reason. They try to stop people from eating meat and wearing clothes made of animal hides. They also try to stop researchers from using animals in their experiments. In pairs, make a list of the advantages and disadvantages of using animals for food, clothing, and research.

Richard Harrington/National Archives of Canada/PA-129942

© PEARSON LONGMAN • REPRODUCTION PROHIBITED

ADVANTAGES	DISADVANTAGES
Fur trapping provides an income for some people.	Some traps are very cruel and animals suffer for a long time.

Share your list with the class.

2. Debate

Divide the class into two teams. One team must argue for the benefits of using animals and the other team must argue for animal rights. Take ten minutes to plan your argument. Choose a speaker for each group. Flip a coin to decide who goes first. Each speaker talks for two minutes. Then, for ten minutes, the teams help the speaker find arguments against what the other team has said. Each team has four minutes to argue their points. The teacher decides which team is most convincing.

3. History of Your Community

Find out about the history of the community in which you live by going to the library or by searching on the Internet. Write a story about your community. Your story should answer the following questions:

• How did your town or city get its name?

• Who were the first European settlers in your area?

• When did the first settlers come?

• When did your community become a city?

• What is the population of your city?

• Was your city ever a trading post?

• Was there a Native village on the site of your community?

• Is there a museum or historical monument in your city that tells about our French and English history?

If there is a museum or historical monument in your city, plan a trip to see it.

4. Famous Historical Figures

Each student in the class can choose one of the following names. Using *The Canadian Encyclopedia,* the library, or the Internet, find out why the person you have chosen is

© PEARSON LONGMAN • REPRODUCTION PROHIBITED

Our English and French Heritage

important in Canadian history. As a class, decide who you think was the most important person.

- Captain James Cook
- Captain George Vancouver
- Anthony Henday
- Alexander Mackenzie
- David Thompson
- Simon Fraser
- Paul Kane
- Radisson & Groseilliers
- Henry Kelsey
- Sieur de la Verendrye
- Jean Talon
- Laura Secord
- Father Lacombe
- Susanna Moodie
- Count Frontenac

THE ST. LAWRENCE RIVER

Native **guides** first led Jacques Cartier, a French explorer, to the St. Lawrence River in 1535. In 1608, Samuel de Champlain, another French explorer, set up a permanent settlement on the St. Lawrence at what is now Quebec City. Throughout the years, the St. Lawrence River has been important for trade and industry. The St. Lawrence Seaway was completed in 1959 as a joint effort of the governments of Canada and the United States. It is a series of locks and canals that connects the Great Lakes to the river. The Seaway lets ships travel approximately 3800 kilometres into the centre of North America.

THE HUDSON'S BAY COMPANY

In 1670, the English King gave the Hudson's Bay Company, a British fur trading firm, control over large parts of Ontario, Quebec, Manitoba, Saskatchewan, Alberta, and the NWT. The Hudson's Bay Company set up nearly one hundred trading posts, many of which are now Canadian cities. The land owned by the company was sold to Canada in 1870. There are Bay department stores in most Canadian cities.

© PEARSON LONGMAN • REPRODUCTION PROHIBITED

Hudson's Bay Company store at Fort Macleod, Alberta

Glenbow Archives NA-622-2

PRE-READING II

PRE-READING II

• Find the Atlantic provinces on a map of North America.

• Find Louisiana in the United States.

• Calculate how many kilometres it is from Halifax, Nova Scotia, to New Orleans, Louisiana.

• How long do you think it would take a person to walk that distance?

• What does it mean to be deported?

READING II
The Acadians

1   The French settlers who came to Nova Scotia in the 1600s were called Acadians. In the 1700s, Britain and France were at war. Although England had control over Nova Scotia after 1713, the English settlers were very worried about the large number of French Acadian farmers in the area. The Acadians claimed to be **neutral**; that is, they promised
5   not to fight the British, or to help France, but the British didn't trust them.

2   In 1755 the British government told the Acadians that they must **swear allegiance** to the English King or be **deported** from Nova Scotia. The Acadians did not want to swear allegiance because they were afraid they would have to fight their own people, the French. They wanted to be left alone to farm.

3   10 The English began to force the Acadians out of the area. Nearly 15 000 Acadians were deported. Many families were split up and people had no choice of where they could go. Some Acadians **escaped** to Quebec and returned to Nova Scotia and New Brunswick when the English and French stopped fighting. Many Acadians moved to Louisiana where they set up new communities. Today there are still **descendants** of
15 the Acadians in Louisiana; they are called Cajuns.

© PEARSON LONGMAN • REPRODUCTION PROHIBITED

COMPREHENSION AND DISCUSSION QUESTIONS

1. Why did the English force the Acadians to leave?

2. Where did the Acadians go?

3. What are the Acadians who moved to Louisiana called today?

4. Acadians became refugees. Where are there refugees today?

LANGUAGE AND CONTACT ACTIVITIES

1. Write a Story

Write a short story about an Acadian family deported to Louisiana. Describe the farm where they lived, how the English forced them out, and the long journey to Louisiana. Some information has been provided for you.

Acadian Deportation

INFORMATION
Who: Jacques and Claudette Hébert and their children François, Isabelle, Luc, Michele.
When: Dinner time, June 21, 1755.
Where: The Hébert farmhouse in Acadia.
What happened: English soldiers came through the door holding guns. They ordered the Héberts to leave. The Héberts had ten minutes to get their things together. The Héberts walked to Louisiana.
Why: The English were afraid of the Acadians.

Write your story using complete sentences. Give your story a title. Exchange your story with someone else. Read your partner's story. Correct any errors you find.

2. Giving Directions using Google Map

A friend of yours is visiting from the country you came from. She wants to go shopping, but you can't go with her because you have to go to school. Using the internet, go to http://maps.google.ca/ and find directions from your house to the closest Bay store. Write out the directions from your house to the Bay. Compare your set of directions with other students' directions. Who lives closest to the Bay? Who lives farthest? How many kilometres is your house from the Bay? How long will it take your friend to get there?

THE UNDERGROUND RAILWAY

Between 1840 and 1860, many Black American **slaves** came to Canada in search of freedom. There was a **network** of people in Canada and the United States who helped the slaves travel safely. This network was called the "Underground Railway". About 30 000 Blacks entered Canada this way. Although they were legally free, they faced discrimination and hardship. Some created their own communities such as Africville in Halifax.

Very few Blacks came to Canada after the United States **abolished** slavery. One reason they didn't come north was the discriminatory medical exams that the Canadian government put into place to keep Blacks out. However, some Black settlers did come to Canada, such as the residents of Amber Valley in Alberta. From 1911 to the 1930s, the majority of people in Amber Valley were Blacks who created a strong and **vibrant** community.

Today there are large numbers of Blacks in Toronto and Montreal, many of whom are not descendants of American Blacks, but who have come in the last forty years from the Caribbean and African countries. Unfortunately, racial discrimination continues to be a problem for Blacks in Canada.

© PEARSON LONGMAN • REPRODUCTION PROHIBITED

Photo by TonyEno.com

The Caribbean community in Toronto celebrates its heritage at the annual Caribana festival.

© PEARSON LONGMAN • REPRODUCTION PROHIBITED

Canadian Issue

Canada: One Country or Many?

Although Canada has been an **independent** country since 1867, there have always been struggles between different groups. In Quebec, for example, there have always been French people who are unhappy with English **dominance**. They think that **separation** from the rest of Canada is the only way to maintain their French **identity**. In the 1960s, the Parti Québécois (PQ), a provincial political party committed to the independence of Quebec, was formed. In 1976, the PQ became Quebec's provincial government. In 1980, the people of Quebec voted to decide whether they wanted to separate from Canada. Although the majority decided not to separate, many Quebecers still wanted to have a separate country. Quebec held another vote in 1995. This time only 51 percent of Quebecers voted to stay in Canada, but because they formed a majority, the province stayed in Canada. Today, there are still many Quebecers who would like to separate.

People from Quebec are not the only ones who want more independence. The First Nations people would like to have more control over their lives. Also, some people in western Canada feel that the federal government has too much control.

Canada is a unique country because it is so big and yet has a small population made up of many different groups of people. There may always be struggles; **national unity** will always be difficult to **achieve**.

Follow-up

Divide into groups of four. Discuss the following questions:

• Do you think Quebec should separate from the rest of Canada? Explain your answer.

• Do you think Quebec will separate from the rest of Canada? Explain.

• If Quebec separates,

  – will there be violence?

  – what will happen to the English people living in Quebec?

  – what will happen to First Nations people living in Quebec?

  – what will happen to immigrants to Quebec?

GLOSSARY OF TERMS

NOUNS

descendant
opposite of ancestor

dominance
powerful influence

guide
someone who shows the way

identity
what a person or thing is

majority
over 50 percent; most

national unity
one identity; shared values within a country

network
group

pelt
animal hide; fur

separation
splitting up

settlers
people who come to live in a new land

slave
a person who is owned by another person

struggles
conflicts

trading post
a place where people exchange goods

trinkets
items such as beads, bracelets, pots and pans

VERBS

to abolish
to do away with, to get rid of, to make illegal

to achieve
to succeed; to get

to deport
to send away

to escape
to get away

to settle
to establish a new home

to swear allegiance
to promise loyalty

ADJECTIVES

independent
self-governing

neutral
neither for nor against

permanent
lasting; not temporary

vibrant
lively, exciting

© PEARSON LONGMAN • REPRODUCTION PROHIBITED

Test Yourself

Our English and French Heritage

MULTIPLE CHOICE

Circle the best answer.

1. Newfoundland was claimed for the King of England in 1497 by _____.
   A) Sir Wilfrid Laurier   C) Pierre Trudeau
   B) Samuel de Champlain   D) Giovanni Caboto

2. The first Canadian city was _____.
   A) Ottawa   C) Toronto
   B) Montreal   D) Quebec City

3. Quebec City was built by _____.
   A) Sir Wilfrid Laurier   C) Jacques Cartier
   B) Samuel de Champlain   D) Giovanni Caboto

4. The French lived by doing all of the following except _____.
   A) hunting   C) trading with the Indians
   B) fishing   D) mining

5. Many Acadians moved to _____ after being deported.
   A) Louisiana   C) New Brunswick
   B) Acadia   D) British Columbia

TRUE/FALSE

Circle *T* if the statement is true. Circle *F* if it is false.

1. Newfoundland was claimed for the King of England in 1497 by Samuel de Champlain. T / F

2. The first Canadian city was Montreal. T / F

3. Quebec City was founded by Wilfrid Laurier. T / F

4. Many Acadians moved to Yukon after being deported from Acadia. T / F

5. The French settlers who came to Nova Scotia in the 1600s were called Acadians. T / F

© PEARSON LONGMAN • REPRODUCTION PROHIBITED

FILL IN THE BLANKS

In the blank, write the word(s) needed to make the sentence complete.

1. The Seven Years' War was a war between _____ and
   _____.

2. The _____ Act of 1774 provided the French people with some
   basic rights.

3. The French settlers who came to Nova Scotia in the 1600s were called
   _____.

4. Some people in Quebec think that the only way to maintain their French identity
   is to _____.

5. Quebec's first vote on separation occurred in _____.

SHORT ANSWER

Answer the following questions.

1. What percentage of people living in Quebec speak French as their first language?

   _____

2. Which Atlantic provinces make up Acadia?

   _____

3. Where did most Acadians move to after being deported from Acadia?

   _____

4. What provincial political party was formed in Quebec in the 1960s?

   _____

© PEARSON LONGMAN • REPRODUCTION PROHIBITED

Chapter 4 Confederation

MATERIALS REQUIRED: Copies of the portion of your telephone directory that lists federal, provincial, and municipal services; a calendar; newspapers; a recording of *O Canada!* (can be found on the Canadian Heritage website).

SKILLS EMPHASIZED: Reading comprehension, discussion, comparing and contrasting, locating information, problem solving, finding the main idea.

TO THE TEACHER: This chapter covers language for making a request or a complaint. It deals with vocabulary related to government services in your community.

SUGGESTED GRAMMATICAL FOCUS POINTS:
Reading I: modals (e.g., *could, should*), prepositions of time (e.g., *in + year, on + date*).
Reading II: prepositions (e.g., *in charge of, responsible for*).

PRE-READING I

- Do you know when Canada became a country?

- What holidays do Canadians celebrate?

- What did you do on Canada Day (July 1)?

- How does your community celebrate Canada Day?

- Why do we celebrate Canada Day?

© PEARSON LONGMAN • REPRODUCTION PROHIBITED

READING I
Canada Becomes a Country

1   Canada became a country on July 1,
1867. The provinces of Quebec, Ontario,
New Brunswick, and Nova Scotia joined
to become a single country. The other
5   provinces and territories joined Canada
after 1867. The last to join was
Newfoundland in 1949. In 2001, the
province of Newfoundland officially
became Newfoundland and Labrador.
10 In 1999, the Northwest Territories were
divided into two territories: Northwest
Territories and Nunavut. The joining
of provinces to make a new country
is called Confederation. Sir John A.
15 Macdonald was the first Prime Minister
of Canada. His picture is on the ten-dollar
bill. We **celebrate** Confederation with a
holiday every year on July 1, Canada Day.

Sir John A. Macdonald was the first
Prime Minister of Canada.

PROVINCES/TERRITORIES	TIME OF ENTRY TO CONFEDERATION
Ontario, Quebec, Nova Scotia, New Brunswick	1867
Manitoba, Northwest Territories (including Nunavut)	1870
British Columbia	1871
Prince Edward Island	1873
Yukon	1898
Alberta, Saskatchewan	1905
Newfoundland & Labrador	1949

© PEARSON LONGMAN • REPRODUCTION PROHIBITED

COMPREHENSION AND DISCUSSION QUESTIONS

1. When did your province join Confederation?

2. What was the last province to join?

3. Who was the first Prime Minister of Canada?

4. Who is the Prime Minister of Canada today?

LANGUAGE AND CONTACT ACTIVITIES

1. National Holidays

Canada has several national holidays as well as provincial and municipal holidays. On these days, most government offices, banks, and schools are closed. Listed below are the national holidays. Find out what dates they are on for this year and learn the purpose of each holiday. You can use a calendar to get the dates; ask a friend or neighbour to tell you what is celebrated on these days if you are not sure.

HOLIDAY	DATE	PURPOSE
Canada Day	July 1	To celebrate Canada's birthday
Christmas		
Thanksgiving		
Good Friday		
Remembrance Day		
New Year's Day		
Victoria Day		
Labour Day		
Boxing Day		
Easter		

2. Other Holidays

People celebrate other holidays in Canada. Compare the national days of all the countries represented in your class. Do your classmates celebrate these days now that they live in Canada? How are these national days celebrated?

There are also special days in Canada that are not official holidays. These include Valentine's Day, St. Patrick's Day, Halloween, Fête Nationale, Mother's Day, Father's Day, birthdays, and wedding anniversaries. People often send each other cards on these days.

Answer the following questions.

• When is Valentine's Day?

• When is St. Patrick's Day?

• When is the Fête Nationale?

• When is Halloween?

• When is Mother's Day?

• When is Father's Day?

• How do Canadians celebrate these special days?

• When is your birthday? How do you celebrate your birthday?

• Are you married? If you are, do you celebrate your wedding anniversary?

© PEARSON LONGMAN • REPRODUCTION PROHIBITED

3. Let's Sing!

Canadians sing the national anthem (see lyrics to *O Canada!* at the side) at hockey games, rodeos, baseball games, and other sporting events. They also sing it at citizenship ceremonies and on Canada Day. Go to the Canadian Heritage website (http://www.pch.gc.ca/) and listen to a recording of *O Canada!* As a class, sing *O Canada!*

Some people feel that the third line in *O Canada*— "True patriot love in all thy sons command"—should be "True patriot love in all of us command" to reflect all Canadians. Other people think that the word "sons" refers to soldiers who have given their lives for Canada. They believe it would be disrespectful to change the words. What do you think?

What is the national anthem of your first country? When do people sing it? What does each line mean?

Canadians celebrating a holiday

THE CANADIAN NATIONAL ANTHEM: *O CANADA!*

O Canada!
Our home and native land!
True **patriot** love in all thy sons command.
With glowing hearts we see thee rise,
The true North strong and free.
From far and wide, O Canada
We stand on guard for thee.
God keep our land **glorious** and free.
O Canada, we stand on guard for thee.
O Canada, we stand on guard for thee.

National Archives of Canada / PA-139073

Louis Riel was a Métis activist in the late 1800s.

LOUIS RIEL

In 1870, the people in what is now Manitoba were deciding whether or not to join Canada. At that time, the majority of people in Manitoba were Native or Métis. Many Native people and Métis did not want Manitoba to join Confederation. They did not believe that Canada would be a good place for them. They wanted a separate country for themselves. Louis Riel, a Métis, led a **rebellion** to stop Manitoba from joining Canada. There was a struggle between the Native people and the European settlers. Riel was defeated and Manitoba joined Confederation. Although he was later **hanged** for **treason**, many Canadians think Riel was a **hero** who fought for aboriginal rights.

© PEARSON LONGMAN • REPRODUCTION PROHIBITED

PRE-READING II

Here are some of the responsibilities of each level of government in Canada.

Responsibilities of the three levels of government

FEDERAL RESPONSIBILITIES	PROVINCIAL RESPONSIBILITIES	MUNICIPAL RESPONSIBILITIES
Citizenship	Health care	Garbage collection
Defence	Education	Recycling
Postal services	Licenses	Water
Employment insurance	Highways	Fire protection
Foreign policy		Streets
Money		City police
Canada Pension		
RCMP		

Canada has three levels of government. The federal government makes laws for the whole country. The provincial and territorial governments make laws that apply in their provinces or territories only. The municipal governments make laws that apply only in their cities or towns. Each level of government has different **responsibilities**.

• What are the three levels of government in Canada?

• Does your first country have different levels of government?

• Who is responsible for building roads in your first country?

• Is there a law in your first country that says what the government is responsible for?

• Have you heard of the Constitution in Canada? What do you know about it?

• What government services have you used in the last month?

© PEARSON LONGMAN • REPRODUCTION PROHIBITED

READING II
The Constitution

When Canada became a country, the British government passed a law called the British North America Act. This Act was Canada's Constitution, or most important law. It outlined the responsibilities of the Canadian federal government and the provincial governments. For example, the federal government is in charge of printing money.
5 No province is allowed to have its own currency. The provincial governments are responsible for education. Each province has its own educational system.

2   The Constitution was kept in
England and could not be changed
without **approval** of the British
10 government. In 1982, Prime Minister
Pierre Elliott Trudeau brought the
Constitution back to Canada.
The Constitution was changed so
that Canada had full control over it.
15 Also, the Canadian Charter of Rights
and Freedoms was made a part of
the Constitution. The Charter
outlines the rights of Canadian
citizens (for example, the right to
20 vote). The Constitution is now
called The Constitution Act, 1982.

Her Majesty Queen Elizabeth II signs the Constitution Act,
1982 as Prime Minister Pierre Elliott Trudeau looks on,

COMPREHENSION AND DISCUSSION QUESTIONS

1. What is a constitution?

2. What was the name of the first Constitution of Canada? Where was it kept?

3. Why was the Constitution brought back to Canada in 1982?

4. What is the name of the new Constitution?

LANGUAGE AND CONTACT ACTIVITIES

1. Locating Government Services in the Phone Book

Working in pairs, use the telephone book to find the numbers for the following services:

• Police

• Fire department

• Citizenship offices

• Passport office

• Immigration office

• Family and social services

• Tourist bureau

Which level of government is responsible for each of these services?

© PEARSON LONGMAN • REPRODUCTION PROHIBITED

2. Problem Solving

Which level of government would you call when

• you want to get a licence for your dog.

• you want to get a driver's licence.

• you want to know how to bring a relative to Canada.

• you want to get a Canadian passport.

• you see someone breaking into your neighbour's house.

• a landlord will not rent an apartment to people from your country.

3. Role Play: Making a Complaint

There is a large **pothole** on Natasha's street. One spring evening, when she was driving home, she didn't see it and Natasha felt a nasty bump when she drove over it. She decided to call the municipal government to complain. Victor works in the department that fixes potholes. Lately, the department has been very busy fixing potholes because the winter was very cold and many roads suffered damage.

Divide the class into two groups. One group will decide what Natasha should say when she phones to complain. The other group will decide what Victor will say. Choose a person from each group to role play the phone call.

4. Writing a Constitution

Working in small groups, write a constitution for your class. Outline the responsibilities of the teacher, the students, and anyone else who comes to your class. Compare your group's constitution with those of others in the class.

© PEARSON LONGMAN • REPRODUCTION PROHIBITED

Canadian Issue

Canadian Unity

In 1982, the Constitution was brought back to Canada. One province, Quebec, decided not to sign it. Over the years, the federal government tried to get Quebec to sign the Constitution. There were several meetings of all the **premiers** and Native leaders. The premier of Quebec wanted Quebec to be recognized in the Constitution as a **distinct** society. In other words, the people of Quebec wanted their language and cultural differences to be recognized by law.

In Charlottetown, an **accord** with proposed changes to the Constitution was drawn up. As part of the accord, Quebec would be recognized as a distinct society and aboriginals would be given more rights. A referendum, or vote, was carried out in the fall of 1992. All Canadians over the age of 18 were asked to vote on whether or not they wanted the proposed changes to the Constitution to be made. The majority of Canadians voted *no*. Many people said that they voted *no* because they were angry with the **politicians**, not because of the issues. Some Native people were very upset, because the changes to the Constitution would have given them more rights to self-government. Many people in Quebec were upset because they thought that the rest of Canada did not want to recognize their unique identity. In 2006, the federal House of Commons voted to recognize the people of Quebec as a nation within Canada. However, Quebec has still not signed the Constitution.

Follow-up

• Do you think that Quebec will ever sign the Constitution?

• Do you think that certain groups in Canada should be given special rights? Why or why not?

GLOSSARY OF TERMS

NOUNS

accord
agreement

approval
permission

hero
a champion, an inspirational person

politician
a person whose business is politics; a person who is interested in affecting how people are governed

pothole
large hole in a road

premier
the leader of a provincial government

rebellion
revolt; uprising

responsibility
duty

treason
betrayal of country; disloyalty

VERBS

to celebrate
to mark a special event

to hang
to kill someone by putting a rope around the neck (note: past tense is "hanged")

ADJECTIVES

distinct
different; unique

glorious
wonderful

patriot
love of country

© PEARSON LONGMAN • REPRODUCTION PROHIBITED

Test Yourself

Confederation

MULTIPLE CHOICE

Circle the best answer.

1. Which was the last province to join Confederation?

   A) Alberta   C) Newfoundland and Labrador

   B) Saskatchewan   D) Nova Scotia

2. Which province below did not join Confederation until after 1867?

   A) Ontario   C) Nova Scotia

   B) Manitoba   D) New Brunswick

3. The provincial governments are responsible for _____.

   A) the post office   C) employment insurance

   B) garbage collection   D) education

4. The municipal governments are responsible for _____.

   A) the RCMP   C) the fire department

   B) immigration   D) postal services

5. Which Prime Minister was responsible for bringing the Constitution back to Canada?

   A) Jean Chrétien   C) John A. Macdonald

   B) Pierre Ellilott Trudeau   D) Mackenzie King

6. Which province did not sign the Constitution Act, 1982?

   A) Quebec   C) Manitoba

   B) Newfoundland and Labrador   D) British Columbia

7. Who was the first Prime Minister of Canada?

   A) Sir John A. Macdonald   C) Pierre Elliott Trudeau

   B) Wilfrid Laurier   D) Mackenzie King

8. Canada became an independent country in _____.

   A) 1776   C) 1982

   B) 1867   D) 1947

TRUE / FALSE

Circle *T* if the statement is true. Circle *F* if it is false.

1. The last province to join Confederation was Newfoundland and Labrador. T / F

2. The federal government is responsible for education. T / F

3. The provincial government is responsible for recycling. T / F

4. The federal government is responsible for post offices. T / F

© PEARSON LONGMAN • REPRODUCTION PROHIBITED

5. The municipal government is responsible for parking tickets. T / F

6. John A. Macdonald was responsible for bringing the Constitution back to Canada. T / F

7. Canada became an independent country in 1867. T / F

8. Saskatchewan joined Confederation in 1905. T / F

9. Nova Scotia joined Confederation in 1867. T / F

10. Manitoba joined Confederation in 1870. T / F

11. Sir Wilfrid Laurier was the first Prime Minister of Canada. T / F

FILL IN THE BLANKS

In the blanks, write the word(s) needed to make the sentence complete.

1. Canada became an official country in _____.

2. _____ is the joining of provinces to make a new country.

3. _____ was the first Prime Minister of Canada.

4. Canadians celebrate Confederation on _____.

5. Remembrance Day is celebrated on _____.

6. Christmas is celebrated on _____.

7. New Year's Day is celebrated on _____.

8. Louis Riel was born in _____ (location).

9. Prime Minister _____ brought the Constitution back to Canada.

MATCHING

Match each province/territory with the year it joined Confederation. The blanks indicate how many provinces joined in each year.

A. British Columbia   1870 ____ ____

B. Alberta   1867 ____ ____ ____ ____

C. Saskatchewan   1905 ____ ____

D. Manitoba   1873 ____

E. Ontario   1898 ____

F. Quebec   1871 ____

G. New Brunswick   1949 ____

H. Nova Scotia

I. Prince Edward Island

J. Newfoundland and Labrador

K. Northwest Territories

L. Yukon

© PEARSON LONGMAN • REPRODUCTION PROHIBITED

MATCH EACH DAY WITH THE CORRECT DATE.

A. Canada Day	____ November 11
B. Christmas	____ December 26
C. Halloween	____ July 1
D. Valentine's Day	____ January 1
E. Remembrance Day	____ December 25
F. New Year's Day	____ February 14
G. St. Patrick's Day	____ October 31
H. Boxing Day	____ March 17

Which level of government is responsible for the following? Fill in the blank with the appropriate letter (*F* for federal, *P* for provincial or *M* for municipal). The first one has been done for you.

_F_ citizenship	____ recycling	____ utilities	____ currency
____ education	____ postal services	____ highways	____ immigration
____ garbage collection	____ defence	____ employment insurance	____ health care

SHORT ANSWER

Answer the following questions.

1. Which four provinces joined together to become Canada in 1867?

_____

2. What is the name of the national holiday of Canada?

_____

3. What is the British North America Act?

_____

4. Briefly describe who Louis Riel was and why he is important in Canada's history.

_____

5. Which two provinces entered into Confederation in 1905?

_____

6. What are the three levels of government in Canada?

_____

7. List three responsibilities of the federal government.

_____

8. List three responsibilities of the provincial government.

_____

9. List three responsibilities of the municipal government.

_____

© PEARSON LONGMAN • REPRODUCTION PROHIBITED

Chapter 5

Tying the Nation Together

© PEARSON LONGMAN • REPRODUCTION PROHIBITED

SKILLS EMPHASIZED: Reading comprehension, discussion, problem solving, expressing an opinion, explaining, reading a schedule, comparing and contrasting, making choices, sequencing, predicting.

TO THE TEACHER: Review discourse markers that indicate sequencing of information.

SUGGESTED GRAMMATICAL FOCUS POINTS:

Reading I: superlatives, to want + someone/something + infinitive (e.g., *to want settlers to move west*).

Reading II: present perfect (with *since, always, already*).

PRE-READING I

- What is the most important form of transportation in the country you are from?

- Have you ever been on a train in Canada? If yes, where did you go?

- How far is it from Vancouver, British Columbia to St. John's, Newfoundland?

- How many people do you think it would take to build a railroad across Canada?

- What areas of Canada would be most difficult for building a railroad?

- How long do you think it took to build the railroad in Canada?

READING I
Building the Country from Sea to Sea

1   After Confederation in 1867, the government of Canada bought land owned by the Hudson's Bay Company
5   (parts of what are now Ontario, Quebec, Manitoba, Saskatchewan, Alberta, and the Northwest Territories). Prime Minister John A. Macdonald
10   wanted British Columbia to join Confederation. He also wanted settlers to move to the West. He and his government promised to build
15   a railway that would go all the way to the Pacific Ocean.

Construction of a railway bridge

Alexander Henderson / National Archives of Canada / PA-164446

2   It was extremely difficult to build the Canadian Pacific Railway. The rocky Canadian
20   Shield in western Ontario and the mountains in Alberta and British Columbia made the job difficult and dangerous. To build the railway, the Canadian
25   government hired a huge **labour force**, including 15 000 workers from China. They started working on the railroad in 1881. When it was
30   finished in 1885, many Europeans began to move to the West.

Canadian Pacific Railway

National Archives of Canada / C-021427

3   The railway made long-distance travel possible.
35   Wheat and other products could be easily transported. Although today most Canadians travel by car or plane, the railroads are still an important
40   method of transporting goods.

Lord Strathcona driving the last spike in the CPR at Craigalachie

British Columbia Archives, Photo #A-01744

© PEARSON LONGMAN • REPRODUCTION PROHIBITED

COMPREHENSION AND DISCUSSION QUESTIONS

1. Why did Sir John A. Macdonald want to build the railroad?

2. How long did it take to build?

3. Which parts of the railroad were the most difficult to build?

4. What were the advantages of having a railroad?

5. Some countries (for example, Japan) have trains that travel up to 200 kilometres an hour. Do you think Canada needs this type of train? If yes, where should these trains be located? Why?

LANGUAGE AND CONTACT ACTIVITIES

1. Transportation Quiz

Answer the following questions.

QUESTION	YES	NO
Have you ever been on a train in Canada?		
Do you drive a car?		
Have you ever been in an accident?		
Have you ever been on a boat on the ocean?		
Have you ever been on a plane? How many flights have you taken?		
Do you get nervous on planes?		
Do you ever get motion sickness?		
Do you know anyone who works in the transportation industry?		
Have you ever been on a **subway**?		
Do you take the bus to class each day?		

Compare your answers with those of a classmate. What do you and your partner have in common? How are you different?

2. Contributions of Immigrants

Immigrants built the railroad and in doing so, helped to **ensure** that British Columbia would join Confederation. What major **contributions** do immigrants make to Canada today? Work in pairs and share your list with others.

3. Win a Trip

You have decided to enter a **contest** to win a two-day vacation. You will be flown to Ottawa or Edmonton to begin your trip. You have to write a paragraph of 100 words explaining why you would like to take one of the following train trips: Ottawa to Kingston, or Edmonton to Jasper. The contest rules state that you must say why you want to go to the place you have chosen and why you want to take the train. Read your entry to the class. The class can decide who should win the trip.

© PEARSON LONGMAN • REPRODUCTION PROHIBITED

PRE-READING II

PRE-READING II

- What wars was Canada in during the 20th century?

- When were the First and Second World Wars?

- Who fought in the First and Second World Wars?

- What was the Cold War?

READING II
Building the Country Beyond the Seas

1   By the early 1900s, Canada stretched from the Atlantic Ocean to the Pacific Ocean. By the start of the 20th century, Canada took a greater role in the world. During the First World War (1914 – 1918), Canada joined Britain, France and other **allies** to defend Europe against German invasion. Nearly one in ten Canadians served in the war. The
5   **capture** of Vimy Ridge in 1917 was a great Canadian achievement. Many have described this event as "the birth of a nation." That is, Canada was seen as a growing power in the world.

2   In the Second World War (1939 – 1945), Canadians again joined with their allies to defeat Japan and Hitler's Nazi Germany. More than one million Canadians served in the army,
10   navy, and air force, fighting battles on the Atlantic, in northwest Europe, in Italy, Hong Kong, and in the air over Britain and Europe. Although nearly 50 000 Canadians were killed, Canada **emerged** from the Second World War as a strong nation, at home and abroad.

3   Since the end of the Second World War, Canada has played a major role in international affairs. During the Cold War, Canada participated in NATO (North Atlantic Treaty
15   Organization), a group of states that promotes and defends democracy. Canada has also participated in many United Nations peacekeeping operations (including the Korean
20   War, Cypress, Haiti, the former Yugoslavia, and Rwanda).

4   After the attacks on September 11, 2001, on the World Trade Center in New York City and the Pentagon in
25   Washington DC, Canada joined U.S. and NATO forces in Afghanistan to **counter** terrorism. Over the years, Canada has grown as a nation and is widely recognized on the world stage.

The Canadian National Vimy Memorial

© PEARSON LONGMAN • REPRODUCTION PROHIBITED

COMPREHENSION AND DISCUSSION QUESTIONS

1. Why was the Battle of Vimy Ridge important?

2. How many Canadians were killed during the Second World War?

3. What is NATO?

4. Canada has a **reputation** as a peacekeeping nation. Do you think this reputation is deserved?

5. Do you think the war against terrorism will ever be won?

LANGUAGE AND CONTACT ACTIVITIES

1. Internet Activity

The History by the Minute website (http://www.histori.ca/minutes/) has one minute movies that show important events in Canadian military history. Go to the website, click on the link *Historica Minutes,* then click on the Military link and watch the videos on Vimy Ridge and on John McCrea.

2. D-Day: Canadians at Juno Beach

In the Second World War, Canadians fought in several key battles. One of the most famous was D-Day at Juno Beach. Search for Juno Beach on the website http://www.members.shaw.ca/junobeach/index.htm or go to Google and find the answers to the following questions:

• When was the invasion of Juno Beach?

• Who fought at Juno Beach?

• How many Canadians fought at Juno Beach?

• Who won the battle?

• Some people have called the Second World War "the last of the good wars." What does this mean? Do you agree?

3. Canada in Conflict

Read the following chart:

CONFLICT	CONSEQUENCE FOR CANADA
Seven Years' War (1756–1763) between England and France	The French were defeated and England gained control of Canada.
War of 1812 between Canada and the United States	The United States was defeated; the border between Canada and the United States was set.
The Riel Rebellion (1869–1870)	Louis Riel and his followers lost; Manitoba joined Confederation.
First World War (1914–1918)	Many Canadian soldiers died protecting their **allies** in Europe.

© PEARSON LONGMAN • REPRODUCTION PROHIBITED

CONFLICT	CONSEQUENCE FOR CANADA
Second World War (1939–1945)	Many Canadian soldiers died protecting Europe's freedom. When the soldiers came home, so many of them married that they started a "baby boom."
The Korean Conflict (1950–1953)	Canadian soldiers died in this war.
Persian Gulf War (1991)	No Canadians died, but many others did.
War against Terrorism after Sept. 11, 2001	Increased fear and more emphasis on national security.

In a group, discuss the following questions:

• Do you think Canada will ever be involved in another war?

• Do you think there will be a war within Canada?

• Have you been in a war?

• Do you think war is necessary?

Canadian Issue

Chinese Canadians

Many Chinese men came to Canada in the nineteenth century to help build the railway. When it was completed, a lot of them stayed, mostly in British Columbia. The federal government at the time would not allow the men to bring their families to Canada unless they paid a head tax. That is, they had to pay a lot of money for each family member. Most men could not afford the tax. Other laws prevented the Chinese from voting and taking certain jobs. It was not until 1947 that Chinese Canadians were given most of the rights enjoyed by other Canadians, but there were still **restrictions** on Chinese immigration that did not change until 1967. Canada has come a long way in the last few **decades**. There is now less discrimination. In 1988, David See-Chi Lam, a Vancouver businessman born in Hong Kong, was

A Chinese work camp

Surveyor-General Édouard Deville / National Archives of Canada / C-016715

© PEARSON LONGMAN • REPRODUCTION PROHIBITED

appointed to the position of Lieutenant Governor (the Queen's representative) in the province of British Columbia. Adrienne Clarkson, who came to Canada as a refugee from Hong Kong during World War Two, became the Governor General of Canada in 1999. As well, in 2006, the Government of Canada apologized for their actions.

Japanese Canadians

By the 1940s, there were over 20 000 Japanese Canadians living in Canada. Most of these people lived in British Columbia. When Pearl Harbor was attacked by Japan in the Second World War, the Canadian government sent Japanese Canadians to work camps in the interior of British Columbia and in Alberta. The government also sold all their property and possessions. After the war, many Japanese Canadians were deported to Japan. Others were relocated east of the Rockies. Some people spoke out against the government's policies and by 1949 Japanese Canadians' rights were restored. For several years, the Japanese Canadian community tried to get the federal government to apologize for the discrimination during the war. In 1988, the federal government apologized and gave some money to those people who were discriminated against.

CANADIAN AND AMERICAN RELATIONS

Sir John A. Macdonald wanted to build the railway to bring people to the west. He was afraid that the west would become part of the United States and it was his dream that Canada would stretch from sea to sea.

Canada and the United States have a great deal in common, but Canadians have always seen themselves as somewhat different from their American neighbours. When the U.S. became independent in 1776, many people who were loyal to the English King moved north to the Canadian colonies. About 40 000 Loyalists came to Canada at this time.

In 1812 the United States went to war with England. They **invaded** the Canadian colonies because they belonged to England. The Americans lost the war. This was the only time that Canada and the USA were at war with each other. At the end of the war, the border between Canada and the USA was set at the 49th **parallel**. The large number of settlers who went west on the railroad in the late 1800s helped to make sure that the border never changed. Since

that time, the United States and Canada have become close friends, although they occasionally have political **disagreements**.

In January 1994, Canada, the United States, and Mexico signed the North American Free Trade Agreement (NAFTA). This **agreement** means that most products can be sold in each of the three countries without **tariffs**.

After the tragedy of September 11, 2001, nations' attitudes toward one another changed. The United States, in particular, was more concerned about the security of its borders. They have made it far more difficult for people to enter or leave their country. Canadians now need a passport to travel to the United States. Canada, too, has tightened its borders. Unfortunately, one of the consequences of September 11 is **racial profiling** and discrimination towards visible minorities. Another result of September 11 has been a war on terrorism and America's attempt to prevent countries in the Middle East from holding or developing weapons of mass destruction.

© PEARSON LONGMAN • REPRODUCTION PROHIBITED

In 2003, the United States went to war with Iraq to stop the development of weapons of mass destruction, to eliminate the ruling regime in Iraq, and to prevent the spread of terrorism. Canada did not participate in the war; this created tension in Canada-U.S. relations.

www.TwoGypsies.com

Cars and trucks line up at Canada/U.S. border.

GLOSSARY OF TERMS

NOUNS

agreement
in politics, a document in which countries share the same understanding about an issue

ally
partner, friend, associate

capture
take over

contest
competition

contribution
donation

decade
ten years

disagreement
a situation in which people or groups do not think or feel the same way about an issue

labour force
worker

parallel (of latitude)
a measure of how far one is from the equator

racial profiling
a kind of discrimination based on racial background, ancestry, or religion

restriction
limit

reputation
name, status

subway
an underground train within a city

tariff
tax on imported goods or products

VERBS

to counter
to oppose

to ensure
to make sure

to emerge
to come out

to invade
to enter and attack

© PEARSON LONGMAN • REPRODUCTION PROHIBITED

Test Yourself

Tying the Nation Together

MULTIPLE CHOICE

Circle the best answer.

1. After Confederation, the Canadian government bought land from _____.
   A) the Americans
   B) the Hudson's Bay Company
   C) Manitoba
   D) the French

2. John A. Macdonald wanted to build the railway because _____.
   A) he needed to provide jobs
   B) he wanted to unite Canada
   C) he liked trains
   D) he wanted to travel

3. In 1812, Canada went to war with _____.
   A) Australia
   B) France
   C) the United States
   D) Bolivia

4. British Columbia joined Confederation because _____.
   A) people there preferred Canada over the United States
   B) it wasn't rich enough to become its own country
   C) people there wanted a train between the east and west
   D) none of the above

5. The work force used to build the Canadian Pacific Railway was largely made up of _____ workers.
   A) immigrant
   B) women
   C) children
   D) none of the above

TRUE/FALSE

Circle *T* if the statement is true. Circle *F* if it is false.

1. The Canadian Pacific Railway was started in 1885. T / F

2. The Canadian Pacific Railway was finished in 1885. T / F

3. The border between Canada and the United States is along the 60th parallel. T / F

4. Many Loyalists moved to Canada after the American Revolution. T / F

5. Canada has had two conflicts with the United States. T / F

6. Canada participated in both the First World War and the Second World War. T / F

© PEARSON LONGMAN • REPRODUCTION PROHIBITED

MATCHING

Canada has been involved in various conflicts throughout history. Match the following conflicts with the dates they began.

A. Korean Conflict   _____ 1991

B. First World War   _____ 1939

C. The Riel Rebellion   _____ 1756

D. War of 1812   _____ 1869

E. Second World War   _____ 1914

F. Seven Years' War   _____ 1812

G. Persian Gulf War   _____ 1950

SHORT ANSWER

Answer the following questions.

1. Why did the government buy land owned by the Hudson's Bay Company?

   _____

2. Why did John A. Macdonald want British Columbia to join Confederation?

   _____

3. Why did John A. Macdonald want to build the Canadian Pacific Railway?

   _____

4. Why was it difficult to build the Canadian Pacific Railway?

   _____

5. List two things that the Canadian Pacific Railway was used for.

   _____

6. Why did many people move to Canada from the United States after the American Revolution of 1776?

   _____

7. When was the border between Canada and the United States established?

   _____

8. What was important about the Battle of Vimy Ridge?

   _____

© PEARSON LONGMAN • REPRODUCTION PROHIBITED

© PEARSON LONGMAN • REPRODUCTION PROHIBITED

Chapter 6
Canada Today: A Diverse Society

SKILLS EMPHASIZED: Reading comprehension, discussion, reading and constructing graphs, designing and conducting a survey, analyzing a survey, writing letters, listing, comparing and contrasting, explaining, reporting information, evaluating, expressing an opinion.

TO THE TEACHER: This chapter incorporates graph reading (pie charts, bar graphs, line graphs, etc.), adjectives, the principles of letter writing, and the names of nationalities (e.g., *France = French, Sudan = Sudanese, Bosnia = Bosnian*). Students will be conducting a survey, so they should focus on vocabulary and phrases for initiating contact (e.g., *"Excuse me, I'm conducting a survey, and I would appreciate your help."*) and for closing conversations (e.g., *"Thank you for your time."*).

SUGGESTED GRAMMATICAL FOCUS POINTS:

Reading I: describing line graphs using verb + adverb + prepositional phrase (e.g., *rose sharply between 1900 and 1910*).

Reading II: modals (e.g., *should, would*), noun clauses.

PRE-READING I

Look at the graph on page 62 and answer the following questions:

• When was the period of greatest immigration to Canada?

• When was the period of least immigration to Canada? Can you guess why?

• Why do you think people came to Canada in the late 1800s?

• Why do they come now?

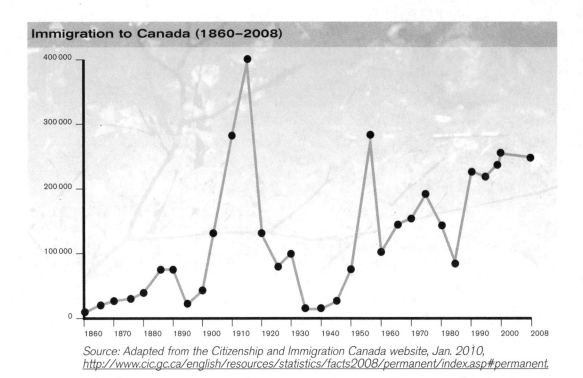

Immigration to Canada (1860–2008)

Source: Adapted from the Citizenship and Immigration Canada website, Jan. 2010,
http://www.cic.gc.ca/english/resources/statistics/facts2008/permanent/index.asp#permanent.

READING I
Immigration Trends

1 There have been several times in Canadian history when large numbers of people
came to this country to start a new life. In the late 1800s, following the completion
of the railway, the federal government **encouraged** Europeans to come to
Western Canada to homestead (farm). Farmland was offered to settlers for free or for
5 a very low price. Many Europeans came to the prairies to look for a better life. Other
immigrants came to search for gold in British Columbia and Yukon. This period
produced the first big wave of immigration to Canada.

A homestead in Canada

J.A. Fletcher / National Archives of Canada / PA-017378

© PEARSON LONGMAN • REPRODUCTION PROHIBITED

2   Just before the First World War (1914–1918), very large numbers of newcomers arrived in Canada. In 1913 alone, more than 400 000 people came to this country.

10 This was the second wave of immigration. After the Second World War (1939–1945), Canada's **economy** grew and people were needed to work in all the new jobs. This was the third period of high immigration to Canada.

3   Today there are still many people coming to Canada from other countries. The table below shows where immigrants came from in 2008.

Immigration to Canada by Source Countries, 2008

COUNTRY	NUMBER OF IMMIGRANTS	PERCENTAGE (%) OF IMMIGRANTS
People's Republic of China	29 336	11.8%
India	24 549	10%
Philippines	23 724	9.6%
United States	11 216	4.5%
United Kingdom	9 243	3.7%
Pakistan	8 052	3.3%
Republic of Korea	7 245	3%
France	6 384	2.6%
Iran	6 010	2.5%
Colombia	4 995	2%
Other Countries	116 489	47%
TOTAL	247 243	100%

Source: Adapted from the Citizenship and Immigration Canada website, Jan. 2010, http://www.cic.gc.ca/english/resources/statistics/facts2008/ permanent/10.asp#countries.

COMPREHENSION AND DISCUSSION QUESTIONS

1. Why did many Europeans come to the West in the late 1800s?

2. When was the second period of high immigration to Canada?

3. Why do people immigrate to Canada today?

4. Why did you immigrate to Canada?

5. Where did the most immigrants come from in 2008?

Mining on Bonanza Creek, Yukon, during the Klondike gold rush

© PEARSON LONGMAN • REPRODUCTION PROHIBITED

Glenbow Archives NA-912-9

LANGUAGE AND CONTACT ACTIVITIES

1. Categories of Immigrants

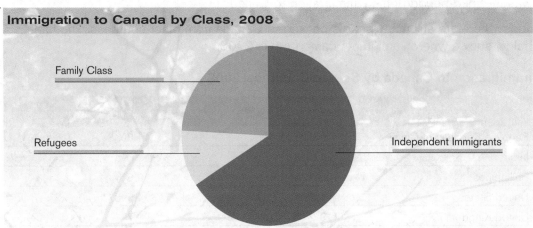

Immigration to Canada by Class, 2008

Family Class

Refugees

Independent Immigrants

Source: Adapted from the Citizenship and Immigration Canada website, Jan. 2010,
http://www.cic.gc.ca/english/resources/statistics/facts2008/permanent/08.asp#cat_source.

As the chart shows, people immigrate to Canada in one of three **categories**: family class (newcomers who are joining family members already in Canada); **independent** class (immigrants who are chosen according to a point system, where points are given for age, occupation, language ability, education, work experience, financial status—this class includes business investors); and refugee class (these are people who would be in danger if they stayed in their first countries).

In pairs or groups, discuss the following questions:

• Where were you when you applied to immigrate?

• How long did you have to wait?

• Could you choose where you wanted to go within Canada?

• Do you have any family here?

• Would you like to sponsor someone to come to Canada?

2. Changes to the Immigration Policy

In 1994, the federal government made some changes to the immigration policy. A greater percentage of newcomers is now in the independent class and fewer family class immigrants are admitted to Canada. The Canada-U.S. Safe Third Country Agreement, implemented in 2004, states that refugee claimants who enter Canada through the U.S. will be turned away. What do you think of these changes?

3. Invite a Guest Speaker to Class

Working together, plan the details of a letter. Invite an immigration official or settlement worker to come to your class to explain the immigration **policy** and to discuss how to

© PEARSON LONGMAN • REPRODUCTION PROHIBITED

sponsor an immigrant to Canada. Be sure to include your class time, dates, location, and the name and telephone number of a contact person from your class.

Make a list of questions that you would want to ask. For example, you might ask the following:

• Who is eligible to sponsor an immigrant?

• How much does sponsoring an immigrant cost?

4. Where Are the Students in Your Class From?

As a class, find out which countries all the students are from.

Write the names of the countries and the number of people from each one on the board.

Add up the total number of students in your class. Calculate the percentage of students from each country.

Example: The following percentages were taken from an ESL class in Vancouver:

• Twenty students were in the class.

• Eight were from China ($8/20 = X/100$, $X = 40$ percent).

• Thus 40 percent of the people in the class came from China.

• Two students came from Phillippines = 10 percent.

• Two students came from Iran = 10 percent.

• Three students came from Korea = 15 percent.

• One student came from Romania = 5 percent.

• One student came from Mexico = 5 percent.

• Two students came from Colombia = 10 percent.

• One student came from India = 5 percent.

The pie graph below shows the percentage of people from each country in the ESL class in Vancouver.

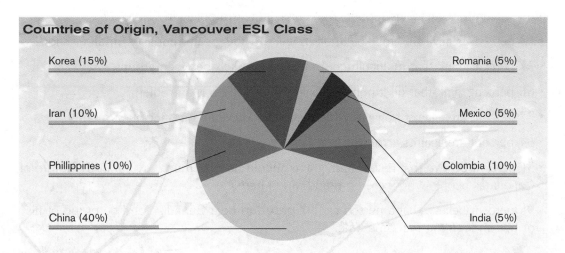

Countries of Origin, Vancouver ESL Class

Korea (15%)
Romania (5%)
Iran (10%)
Mexico (5%)
Phillippines (10%)
Colombia (10%)
China (40%)
India (5%)

© PEARSON LONGMAN • REPRODUCTION PROHIBITED

Now draw a pie graph of your own class. Once you have found the percentage of students from every country in your class, draw a large circle on the board. Fill in the pie graph.

How is your class different from the sample ESL class in Vancouver?

PRE-READING II

• What is multiculturalism?

• Do you think multiculturalism is a good thing? Why or why not?

• What do you think Canadians who were born in Canada think about multiculturalism?

READING II
Multiculturalism

1   In 1988, the Canadian Multiculturalism Act was passed. The Act states that the government of Canada respects and supports cultural and racial **diversity**. People are encouraged to keep and share their cultural and linguistic **heritage**. This means that all Canadians should have equal opportunities, no matter where they come from. They
5   should also be able to celebrate their ethnic **traditions** and speak in their own language as well as in English or French.

2   Canada is often called a cultural **mosaic**, a place where people from many countries can adapt to Canadian life and yet keep the traditions from their first culture. A few years ago, the federal government **surveyed** Canadians. People were asked about their
10   views on multiculturalism and about their **attitudes** toward different cultures in Canada. Here are some of the results from the survey:

• 61 percent of Canadians support the multiculturalism policy in Canada.

• 73 percent believe that multiculturalism will provide greater equality for all Canadians.

• 37 percent think that multiculturalism creates conflicts between groups.

15 • 66 percent think that discrimination against non-whites is a problem.

• 77 percent are against polygamy (marriage to more than one person at a time).

• 64 percent are against **arranged marriages**.

• 51 percent believe that recent immigrants should have as much say about the future of Canada as people who were born and raised here.

20 • 95 percent believe that a person can be **proud** to be a Canadian and be proud of his or her **ancestry** at the same time.

© PEARSON LONGMAN • REPRODUCTION PROHIBITED

COMPREHENSION AND DISCUSSION QUESTIONS

1. What is the Multiculturalism Act?

2. What does it mean to say that Canada is a mosaic?

3. Do you agree with the ideas in the Multiculturalism Act?

4. Do you think that the multiculturalism policy is good for Canada? Why or why not?

5. Do people from your first country maintain their heritage in Canada?

6. What do you think of arranged marriages?

7. If you have children, do you want them to carry on the traditions from their first country? If yes, do you think this will be difficult? Explain.

LANGUAGE AND CONTACT ACTIVITIES

1. Survey of Attitudes Toward Multiculturalism

Conduct a survey to find out what people think about multiculturalism. Each class member should ask five people (not members of the class) to answer the following questions. Record their answers.

	YES	NO
1. Do you support the multiculturalism policy of Canada?		
2. Do you think that multiculturalism creates conflicts between groups?		
3. Do you think that discrimination against non-whites is a problem?		
4. Do you think that newcomers should have as much to say about the future of Canada as people who were born and raised here?		
5. Do you think that Canada should increase the level of immigration?		

As a class, put your results from the survey together. How many people in total answered the survey? Calculate the percentage of people who answered *yes* or *no* to each of the questions and fill out the following chart:

QUESTION	PERCENTAGE YES	PERCENTAGE NO
Question 1		
Question 2		
Question 3		
Question 4		
Question 5		

Individually, write a report of the results, including information from each question. Give your thoughts on the results. Give your report to another person in the class while you read his or her report.

© PEARSON LONGMAN • REPRODUCTION PROHIBITED

Canada is a multicultural nation.

Canadian Issue

Conflict and Multiculturalism

Many people come to Canada because of conflict in their countries. They may have been at war with another country or with a particular group of people within their own country. Sometimes newcomers have trouble forgetting the **hostility** they feel towards the other group and may continue to have conflicts with members of that group here in Canada. In a survey conducted in Edmonton, ESL students were asked the following question: "What do you think about people bringing their conflicts to Canada?" Here are some of their comments:

"We live in Canada now. People who were our enemies are not our enemies here." — *Woman from Iraq*

"People come here to get away from war, not to make war." —*Man from El Salvador*

"We should find a middle way; there should be general rules for everyone, and we must respect Canadian law."—*Man from Romania*

"It is bad to bring conflicts from your home country. People should get along even with their enemies here." —*Woman from Bosnia*

"Canada is a peaceful country. Immigrants should respect that." —*Woman from Korea*

Follow-up

• Do you spend time outside of class with people outside your own ethnic group?

• What do you think about bringing conflicts to Canada? Are there circumstances when it is acceptable?

• Do you think it is possible for enemies to become friends in a new country?

• Do you think that Canadian-born people understand the problems of newcomers?

© PEARSON LONGMAN • REPRODUCTION PROHIBITED

Canadian Issue

Teenage Immigrant Angst

Some immigrant teenagers find it difficult to adjust to their new lives in Canada. Some never wanted to leave their countries in the first place while others were disappointed after they arrived. A group of immigrant high school students were asked about their adjustment to Canadian life. Here are some of their comments:

"I cried for the first three months. I didn't understand English, school was difficult, and I missed my friends back home."

"My parents were very angry when I found a Canadian girlfriend."

"My parents made me study all the time."

"I feel a lot of guilt. My parents moved here to make a better life for me but I wish we'd stayed where we were."

"My parents have told me they will find me a husband. I want to choose my own."

"My parents don't understand how it is for me. They won't let me go out with my friends or do after-school activities."

"I feel like I live a double life. I'm two people–one at home and one at school."

Follow-up

• What do you think are the most serious problems for teenagers and their parents?

• Do you think immigrant teenagers have different problems than Canadian-born teenagers?

• How can these problems be resolved?

DISCRIMINATION

In one school, fourteen students in an ESL class were asked whether there is discrimination now in Canada. Nine people said that there is some discrimination on the basis of sex, skin colour, nationality, and language skills. How many people in your class have been discriminated against?

Here are some cases of discrimination.

Some religions require that people dress in a certain way; for example, **Sikh** men wear **turbans**. In 1994, some **branches** of the Royal Canadian Legion, which does not allow its members to wear headgear, decided not to let anyone inside wearing a turban. The Legion is a social club for war **veterans** and their families and friends. The Legion members argued that it is a sign of respect to remove headgear when entering the Legion. They say that allowing people to wear a turban would break an important **tradition**. What they were asking, however, was for turban-wearers to break an important requirement of their religion in order to follow this tradition. Many Sikhs fought in the Second World War and feel that they should have equal access to the Legion halls.

© PEARSON LONGMAN • REPRODUCTION PROHIBITED

World events often **trigger** discrimination. After September 11, 2001, many Arab and Muslim Canadians experienced discrimination even though they had nothing to do with the terrorist attacks in the United States.

Women in Canada have been fighting for equal rights for a long time. Do you think that women in Canada have the same job opportunities as men?

When ESL students were asked whether women should have equal rights, twelve out of fourteen said yes; the two who said no were both men.

- Do you think that women should have equal rights?

- Do you think that women do have equal rights?

- In your class, is there a difference between the percentage of men and the percentage of women who think women should have equal rights?

Some people are discriminated against because of their sexual identity. However, it is a Canadian value to recognize diversity and **gay** rights in particular. In 1967, Pierre Elliott Trudeau argued for the decriminalization of homosexuality, saying, "There is no place for the state [government] in bedrooms of the nation." In 1969, Bill C-150 passed. It was no longer against the law to be a homosexual. In 2005, same sex marriage became legal in Canada. Several elected officials at all levels of government have been openly gay. For example, Scott Brison, a Member of Parliament from Nova Scotia, is a popular politician who is married to his same sex partner. Although there is greater acceptance of gays and **lesbians**, they still face discrimination by a minority.

Are people often openly gay or lesbian in your country?

- In your province are there laws to protect gay and lesbian people from discrimination?

- Why do you think people sometimes try to hide their sexual **orientation**?

- Think of some other examples of discrimination in Canada. What do you think can be done about this problem?

GLOSSARY OF TERMS

NOUNS

ancestry
the cultural group from which you are descended

angst
anxiety, worries, distress

arranged marriage
a marriage that results when parents choose a husband or wife for their child

attitude
a way of feeling or thinking about someone or something

branch
a part of a large organization

category
class or group

diversity
differences; variety

economy
the system by which a country's wealth is produced and used

heritage
cultural background

gay
homosexual

hostility
anger; animosity

lesbian
a homosexual woman

mosaic
a collection of separate pieces that form a whole

orientation
the direction of a person's thoughts, activities, or beliefs

policy
a course of action

© PEARSON LONGMAN • REPRODUCTION PROHIBITED

Sikh
a person who belongs to a religion
called Sikhism

trend
pattern

tradition
beliefs, customs from the past

turban
headgear; Sikh men must wear one

veteran
someone who has fought in a war

ADJECTIVES

independent
free from authority or control

proud
feeling satisfaction and pleasure about
something connected to oneself

VERBS

to encourage
to support

to sponsor
to pay for

to survey
to ask several questions
of a number of people

to trigger
to start

Test Yourself

Canada Today: A Diverse Society

MULTIPLE CHOICE

Circle the best answer.

1. There were _____ waves of immigration to Canada.
   A) two   C) four
   B) three   D) five

2. The Canadian Multiculturalism Act was passed in _____.
   A) 1982   C) 1867
   B) 1988   D) 1905

3. Many of the immigrants who arrived in Canada during
   the first wave were _____.
   A) Chinese   C) Australian
   B) African   D) European

4. Immigrants can enter Canada under which of the following categories?
   A) family class   C) refugee
   B) independent   D) all of the above

5. The Canadian mosaic is a _____.
   A) traditional food dish   C) collection of distinct cultures
   B) traditional dance   D) political party

© PEARSON LONGMAN • REPRODUCTION PROHIBITED

TRUE/FALSE

Circle *T* if the statement is true. Circle *F* if it is false.

1. Canada is often called a mosaic. T / F

2. People came to Canada in the late 1800s to homestead. T / F

3. Farmland was very expensive one hundred years ago. T / F

4. An immigrant can enter Canada as an independent. T / F

5. The highest number of immigrants entered Canada in 1945. T / F

6. The majority of Canadians support immigration to Canada. T / F

FILL IN THE BLANKS

In the blank, write the word(s) needed to complete the sentence.

1. The Canadian Multiculturalism Act was passed in _____.

2. Because of its multicultural nature, Canada is often called a _____.

3. The _____ wave of immigration occurred during the nineteenth century.

4. _____ made up the majority of immigrants during the third wave of immigration.

SHORT ANSWER

1. Why did the federal government encourage large numbers of people to move to Western Canada in the 1800s?

   _____

2. Independent immigrants are chosen by a point system. List three things for which they are given points.

   _____

3. When was the greatest period of immigration to Canada?

   _____

4. Why did so many people come to Canada in the late 1800s?

   _____

© PEARSON LONGMAN • REPRODUCTION PROHIBITED

Chapter 7

What Do Canadians Do?

© PEARSON LONGMAN • REPRODUCTION PROHIBITED

MATERIALS REQUIRED: Classified section of the newspaper, sample résumés and cover letters, sample application forms, a few decks of cards.

SKILLS EMPHASIZED: Reading comprehension, discussion, reading classified ads, letter writing, writing a résumé, sequencing, listing, giving instructions, making choices, explaining.

TO THE TEACHER: Go over vocabulary for occupations, industries, and leisure activities. Review methods of sequencing and giving instructions.

SUGGESTED GRAMMATICAL FOCUS POINTS:
Reading I and Reading II: future (*will*), imperatives.

PRE-READING I

Distribution of Employment (2009)

INDUSTRY	PERCENT EMPLOYED
Agriculture	1.9
Forestry, Fishing, Mining, Oil & Gas, Utilities	2.7
Construction	7.0
Manufacturing	10.5
Trade	15.7
Transportation & Warehousing	4.9
Finance, Insurance, Real Estate	6.7

INDUSTRY	PERCENT EMPLOYED
Professional, Scientific & Technical Services	7.1
Educational Services	7.1
Health Care & Social Assistance	11.6
Information, Culture & Recreation	4.7
Accommodation & Food Services	6.2
Public Administration	5.5
Management of Companies & Support Services	3.8
Other Services	4.6

Source: Adapted from the Statistics Canada website, Jan. 2010, http://www40.statcan.ca/l01/cst01/labor21a-eng.htm.

• What kinds of jobs do the majority of working Canadians have?
• What is your job?
• Which category in the chart above fits your job?
• What is the main type of employment in your city or town? In your province?
• What kind of work did you do before you came to Canada?
• What is the main source of employment in the country you came from?

READING I
Working Life in Canada

For hundreds of years, most people in Canada made their living from working with natural resources. Because much of the country is covered with trees, forestry is one of Canada's most important industries. Agriculture is important in all the provinces in Canada. Mining is done throughout the country, and large oil and gas deposits are
5 found in Alberta, Saskatchewan, and off the coast of Newfoundland. The Canadian fishing industry has always been important, but recently there has been a lot of concern about overfishing on both the Atlantic and Pacific coasts. There is a fear that all the codfish in the east and the salmon in the west may disappear.

A farm in Manitoba

Canadian Tourism Commission/
Commission canadienne du tourism

© PEARSON LONGMAN • REPRODUCTION PROHIBITED

A **log boom** in Lethbridge, Alberta   Oil production in Alberta

2   Although much of Canada's economy still depends on agriculture, forestry, mining,
10   **oil refining**, fishing, and manufacturing, most Canadians today live in cities and
     work in service occupations (office work, education, health, transportation, tourism,
     food services, etc.). In the future, there will be more work in high **technology**
     industries. The fastest growing industries are in areas such as computers,
     communications, medicine, and the environmental sector.

3 15 There have been several changes to the workplace in the last twenty-five years in
     Canada. One of the most important changes concerns the number of women who
     work outside the home. A majority of adult women now have jobs. In more than half
     of all two-parent families, both parents work. Another change is that twenty-five years
     ago, a person could expect to stay in the same job for his or her whole **career**.
20   Today, people often find that they have to change jobs several times before
     retirement. They may have to learn new skills as they change jobs. In the near
     future, Canada will need more workers who are well educated. Also, now there
     are many more part-time jobs than ever before.

4   In the future, more and more people will work at home. The number of jobs that
25   involve the use of computers is growing. Many people will not need to go to an
     office to do their work. Already some people do almost all of their work at home;
     that is, they telecommute. They check with their office by telephone or by fax or
     e-mail and they send their work to the office by computer.

5   Many immigrants to Canada don't know what kind of work they will find here. It is
30   sometimes very difficult for them to get jobs in the same occupation they had in their
     own country. Immigrants who have been here for a long time have some advice for
     newcomers. They say that new immigrants need to be **patient** and **persistent**.
     It can be **frustrating** because most newcomers are **underemployed** in the
     beginning. They do not make as much money as they thought they would, and they
35   are disappointed with the jobs they can find. However, many people eventually go
     back to school or find a job connected to their occupation.

© PEARSON LONGMAN • REPRODUCTION PROHIBITED

Glenbow Archives NA-864-3

Provincial Archives of Alberta, Photo P1199

COMPREHENSION AND DISCUSSION QUESTIONS

1. What are Canada's most important industries?

2. Why is fishing a concern on the Atlantic and Pacific coasts?

3. What kinds of jobs do most Canadians work at today?

4. How has the role of women changed in the job market?

5. What kind of job would you like to have in Canada?

6. Do you need any extra education or training to get the job you want?

LANGUAGE AND CONTACT ACTIVITIES

1. Canada's Industries and Resources

Look at the chart below and answer the following questions.

• Which region do you live in?

• What industries and resources are most common where you live?

• What are the main industries and resources in the country you come from?

REGION	PROVINCE OR TERRITORY	INDUSTRIES AND RESOURCES
West Coast	British Columbia	Forestry, Fishing, Tourism, Fruit Farms, Cattle Ranches
The Prairies	Alberta	Oil & Gas, Wheat, Cattle, Tourism
	Saskatchewan	Wheat, Mining (potash)
	Manitoba	Wheat, Hydroelectricity
Central Canada	Ontario	Manufacturing, Mining (nickel, gold, zinc, copper), Fruit, Tourism
	Quebec	Manufacturing, Hydroelectricity, Tourism, Mining, Dairy Farms
Atlantic Provinces	New Brunswick	Forestry, Food Processing
	Nova Scotia	Fishing, Mining, Tourism
	Prince Edward Island	Potato Farms, Tourism
	Newfoundland & Labrador	Fishing, Oil
The North	Yukon	Fur, Mining, Oil & Gas, Arts & Crafts
	Northwest Territories	
	Nunavut	

© PEARSON LONGMAN • REPRODUCTION PROHIBITED

2. Job Advertisements

Many people look for jobs in the classified ads in the newspaper. Some sample advertisements are shown below.

• What kinds of jobs are being advertised here?

• How many of these jobs require experience?

• How many jobs require a **résumé**?

• Do you think these jobs pay well? Explain your answer.

• Which job do you think pays the most? Why?

• Do you qualify for any of these jobs?

> Exp'd waitress/er needed for drive-through restaurant. Good wage, call Sam, 358-2987

> We require salespeople for our busy retail stores. If you are a self starter, hard working individual and want a salary based on your performance, e-mail cover letter and résumé to: carpetmania@123.com

> Carpenters, exper. Submit résumé to Kelsey's Interiors 87 Madison St. R3C 3J1

> PAINTERS
> High quality and high production skills req. FT
> Fax: (340) 775-6632
> Attn: Jack or
> E-mail: jack@paintersplus.com

3. Job Interest Quiz

On the Internet, go to http://jobfutures.ca/en/ and take the job interest quiz. What job does the program say you are most suited for?

4. Finding a Job

Find the classified ad section in your newspaper.

• What kinds of jobs are available?

• Some newspapers have a special section called a *careers section*. What is the difference between the jobs advertised in the careers section and the jobs in the classifieds?

There are also many jobs advertised on the internet. Some large companies advertise jobs on their own websites but there are also websites specifically for employment. One Canadian employment website is Workopolis (http://www.workopolis.com/). Go to Workopolis and find out:

• How many accounting jobs are there in Calgary, Alberta?

• Are there any jobs available where you live in your occupation?

© PEARSON LONGMAN • REPRODUCTION PROHIBITED

5. Writing a Cover Letter and a Résumé

Look again at the job ads in your newspaper or on the Workopolis website. Pick one that asks for a résumé. Write a cover letter and a résumé to apply for the job, following the examples given here:

Sample Cover Letter

Rodrigo Sanchez
83 Oak Drive #6
Ottawa ON
K1A 2Z3

April 15, 2010

Joe Jeffries
Carpet Mania
905 Barrington
Ottawa ON
K1A 0N5

Dear Mr. Jeffries:

I would like to apply for the job of salesperson for Carpet Mania. I have enclosed my résumé. I am a hard worker and I think I could make a good contribution to your store. I **look forward to** hearing from you.

Sincerely,

Rodrigo Sanchez

Rodrigo Sanchez

© PEARSON LONGMAN • REPRODUCTION PROHIBITED

Sample Résumé

Rodrigo Sanchez
83 Oak Drive # 6
Ottawa, ON
K1A 2Z3

Education: (List the years, the training, and the schools that you attended.)

Work Experience: (List all relevant work experience, dates, names of companies, locations, and job responsibilities.)

Skills: (List any skills you have that will be useful for the advertised job.)

References: (List the names, addresses, and phone numbers of two or three people who can say that you are a good worker. The best **references** are former employers, but if you do not have a former employer in Canada, ask your teacher for a reference.)

---

6. Filling Out an Application Form

Many employers ask people to fill out application forms. These forms are different from one company to the next, but they all ask for your name and address, your Social Insurance Number (SIN), your previous education, and work experience. Fill out the sample form on page 80 with your personal information.

© PEARSON LONGMAN • REPRODUCTION PROHIBITED

APPLICATION FORM

Personal Information

Name: _____ SIN: _____

Address: _____
      apt. #   street

_____
      city   province   postal code

Tel. # (h) _____ (b) _____

Previous Education

Schools Attended	Location (city, country)	Month/Year from_____ to_____	Degree

Previous Employment

Name, Address, Tel. # of Employer Job Dates Reason for Leaving

_____

_____

_____

Signature _____ Date _____

© PEARSON LONGMAN • REPRODUCTION PROHIBITED

TEMPORARY FOREIGN WORKERS (TFWS)

In recent years, Canada has experienced severe shortages of people for certain jobs. In response, employers have asked the government to let them bring in temporary foreign workers. Some of these people are in high-end jobs, such as nursing and teaching at universities, while others work in the hotel and agriculture industries. There have been some problems with the TFW program. First, there are **unscrupulous** recruiters, who promise jobs in exchange for large sums of money. Sometimes workers arrive and no such job exists. In other cases, employers treat their TFWs badly and pay them very little. The provincial and federal governments are creating laws to deal with these problems.

7. Minimum Wage in Canada

Choose one person in the class to call the offices of Canada Employment. Find out what the minimum wage is in your province. Is there a minimum wage in your former country? Is it more or less than the minimum wage in your province? Do you think a minimum wage is a good idea? Why or why not?

PRE-READING II

- Do you play any sports?

- Do you have any hobbies?

- Have you ever been to a hockey game?

- Have you ever bought a lottery ticket? If yes, have you ever won anything?

READING II
Leisure Life in Canada

In their **leisure time**, Canadians enjoy the outdoors. In the summertime, people like to swim, fish, garden, bicycle, and walk. Many people go camping and hiking for a few days in a provincial or national park. In the winter, a lot of people skate, toboggan, or ski. But the most popular winter sport is hockey; some people play it but many more watch it
5 on TV. Watching television is the most popular leisure activity of all. On average, Canadians watch more than three hours of TV a day. Some people spend a lot of time in front of a computer screen either playing video games or **surfing the Net**.

Canadians enjoy the outdoors in the summer.

© PEARSON LONGMAN • REPRODUCTION PROHIBITED

Caron Rollins

Caron Rollins

2   Another very popular activity is gambling.
     Some people buy lottery tickets and dream
10   of what they will do if they win the
     jackpot. Other people go to casinos or
     bingo halls and play to win. Most of the
     time they actually lose more money than
     they make, but they have a good time.
15   Unfortunately, some people become
     addicted to gambling. They build up large
     debts and often develop serious family
     problems because of their addiction.

Canadians enjoy skating outdoors in the winter.

COMPREHENSION AND DISCUSSION QUESTIONS

1. What is the most popular leisure activity in Canada?

2. What are some sports that people play in the winter? In the summer?

3. What are three types of gambling that Canadians like?

4. Have you ever bought a lottery ticket?

5. What would you do if you won a million dollars?

6. Have you tried any winter sports here in Canada?

7. Do you watch hockey on TV? Do you watch football on TV?

8. Are there any TV programs in your first language in your city or town?

9. What is your favourite leisure activity?

10. Do you ever surf the Net? What is your favourite website?

11. Did you watch any of the Vancouver 2010 Olympic Games?

LANGUAGE AND CONTACT ACTIVITIES

1. Card Game

Many Canadians like to play cards or board games such as Scrabble. Young people often learn games when they are very little. A popular card game that parents play with their children is called Go Fish. This game can be played by two or more people. Here are the instructions for playing Go Fish:

1. Shuffle the deck.

2. Deal seven cards to each player.

3. Look at your cards; then sort them by number. For example, put all the sixes together and all the kings together.

Provincial Archives of Alberta, Photo J3021

© PEARSON LONGMAN • REPRODUCTION PROHIBITED

4. If you have four of any number, place them face up on the table. Now you are ready to play. The goal of the game is to get complete sets of a number (all four), put the sets down, and run out of cards before anyone else.

5. Ask any other player for a card that you want. For example, call out, "Do you have any eights?" You can only ask for cards that you have at least one of.

6. If the other player has the cards you ask for, he or she has to give them to you and you can ask for something else. If the other player does not have the cards you asked for, he or she says "Go fish." You then draw a new card from the deck.

7. The next player takes his or her turn. The game ends when one person has put down all of his or her cards and has no cards left.

Write a set of instructions for a game or sport that you played in the country you came from. Show the students in the class how to play this game.

2. Camping

You are going to go camping for two days. It is the middle of the summer. In pairs, decide the following: Where will you go? What items will you bring with you? What kind of food will you take?

CANADIAN FESTIVALS

Several Canadian communities have an active theatre and music scene all year round. Most major cities have a symphony orchestra and opera is also popular. As well, there are many festivals, which are short events with many different performers. There are jazz, blues, and country music festivals in several places, but the largest musical events are folk festivals. Winnipeg, for instance, has had a summer folk festival for the past thirty years with performers from all over the world. These are family gatherings—people of all ages find folk festivals enjoyable.

The oldest theatre festival is in Stratford, Ontario. For over fifty years, people have gone there to see plays by Shakespeare and other well-known playwrights. Many Canadians also go to Fringe Festivals to see plays in the summer. At a Fringe Festival, people can see many different types of plays—the atmosphere is like a party. For many years, there was only one Fringe Festival, and it was located in Edinburgh, Scotland. Then Edmonton, Alberta adopted the idea and developed the first and what is now the largest Fringe Festival in North America. Other Canadian cities and towns have **followed suit** and now have their own Fringe Festivals.

Another well-known festival takes place in Toronto every summer. Caribana started in 1967 with a celebration of West Indian communities who wanted to share their culture with people in their adopted homeland. Many cities now have celebrations in which Canadians from different backgrounds celebrate their heritage.

Most festivals take place in the summer, but some occur in the winter months. The Quebec City Winter Carnival is the largest winter festival anywhere. For two weeks in February people **flock** to **parades** each night and to dogsled races, canoe races on the ice, and **snow sculpture** events each day.

© PEARSON LONGMAN • REPRODUCTION PROHIBITED

Caron Rollins

The Edmonton Folk Festival

Canadian Issue

The Changing Face of Canada

Over the last few decades there has been a rise in the divorce rate in Canada. Single-parent and blended families are becoming very common. Some children may grow up with several step-relations in their lives while others live with only one parent.

• More women are working outside the home than ever before. As a result, there is a great need for daycare for children.

• After the Second World War, many soldiers came home, married, and had families. Children born in the post-war period (1947 – 1966) were called "baby boomers". They were called boomers because there were more babies than ever before. The first of the baby boomers are now becoming senior citizens. Some people worry that the health care system will not be able to accommodate the high number of baby boomers needing health care in the future.

• Although there are many different religions represented in Canada (Judaism, Islam, Buddhism, etc.), Christianity has the most members. Over the last few decades, the traditional Christian churches (Catholic, Anglican, Presbyterian, United) have lost significant numbers of members. Many Canadians say that they have religious beliefs, but they are not interested in going to a place of worship (e.g., a church).

Follow-up

• Why do you think that more and more Canadians are getting divorced?

• Do you think married couples should stay together no matter what?

• Do you think the government should provide funds for daycare, or is this an individual responsibility?

• Why do you think fewer people are going to church?

© PEARSON LONGMAN • REPRODUCTION PROHIBITED

GLOSSARY OF TERMS

NOUNS

career
the general course of a person's working life; career also means chosen area of occupation

leisure time
time when a person is not working; free time

log boom
a chain cable or line of timber used to keep logs from floating away

oil refining
processing oil to make it usable

parade
an event where people march or ride in a vehicle down the street while other people watch

reference
the name of a person who can speak on one's behalf

résumé
a statement of a person's work experience and educational qualifications

retirement
the end of one's career

snow sculpture
a carving made of ice and snow

technology
the application of scientific knowledge

VERBS

to flock to
to gather in great numbers at a location
to follow suit
to do the same thing
to look forward to
to anticipate; to be excited about
to surf the Net
to visit many sites on the Internet

ADJECTIVES

addicted
feeling dependent on something and spending a great deal of time on it
frustrating
maddening; disappointing
patient
willing to wait
persistent
continuing to try despite opposition
underemployed
having a job that does not make use of one's skills and education
unscrupulous
dishonest, corrupt

© PEARSON LONGMAN • REPRODUCTION PROHIBITED

Test Yourself

What Do Canadians Do?

TRUE/FALSE

Circle *T* if the statement is true. Circle *F* if it is false.

1. Agriculture is an important industry in Canada today. T / F

2. In most Canadian families, only one of the two parents work. T / F

3. Many Canadians today have more than one job before they retire. T / F

4. More people will work at home in the future. T / F

5. Jobs in Canada in the future will require more advanced education. T / F

6. Single-parent families are not very common in Canada. T / F

7. Fewer women have jobs now than before. T / F

8. Most Canadians like going to a place of worship. T / F

SHORT ANSWER

Answer the following questions.

1. List two natural resources found in British Columbia.

   _____

2. List two industries found in Prince Edward Island.

   _____

3. List two industries found in Quebec.

   _____

4. List two main industries in Alberta.

   _____

5. List two main industries in Ontario.

   _____

6. List two main industries in New Brunswick.

   _____

7. What is one of the most important changes that has happened in
   the workplace in Canada?

   _____

8. List four activities that Canadians enjoy doing in the summer.

   _____

9. List four activities that Canadians enjoy doing in the winter.

   _____

10. What religion has the most members in Canada?

   _____

© PEARSON LONGMAN • REPRODUCTION PROHIBITED

Chapter 8

Canada in a Global World

© PEARSON LONGMAN • REPRODUCTION PROHIBITED

MATERIALS REQUIRED: Pictures of environmental problems.

SKILLS EMPHASIZED: Reading comprehension, finding the main idea, preparing an outline and an essay.

TO THE TEACHER: This chapter introduces many new vocabulary words. Supplement the readings and activities with exercises in which students use and define the new terms. Review discourse markers related to cause and effect (e.g., *so, as a result, consequently, because*).

SUGGESTED GRAMMATICAL FOCUS POINTS:

Reading I: type I conditional (e.g., *if we continue to cut down thousands of trees, there will be global warming; if you do …., you will ….*), making predictions using *will*.

Reading II: time clauses with *when*.

PRE-READING I

• What is a greenhouse?

• How does a greenhouse stay warm?

• What do you think are the most serious environmental problems in the world? In Canada?

• Have you heard of climate change? Have you heard of global warming?

• Which countries contribute the most to global warming?

READING I
Environmental Issues

1 The environment has become an important issue in Canada and other parts of the world. Many scientists say that if we don't change our way of living, we will **destroy** the world. What happens in one country can affect the rest of the world.

2 One issue that has received a great deal of attention is climate change. One aspect
5 of climate change is global warming. Many scientists believe that the whole earth is becoming a **giant greenhouse**. The earth is surrounded by a blanket of gases called the atmosphere. The gases act like the glass in a greenhouse, trapping the heat from the sun. Recently, there has been a **significant** increase in certain gases, especially carbon dioxide, methane, and **chlorofluorocarbons**; these gases trap heat. Consequently,
10 the average temperature of the earth is rising, a trend called global warming.

3 Global warming is caused by the burning of fuels such as oil, coal, wood, and gas; deforestation (the cutting down of forests); vehicle exhaust; **fertilizers**; rotting garbage; and cattle digesting food. In fact, most things that consume energy
15 contribute to the problem (e.g., air conditioning, heating, driving, and manufacturing). Canada has one of the worst records of the **industrialized nations** for
20 producing greenhouse gases.

A power plant polluting the air

4 Global warming results in frightening consequences to the climate. A hotter earth means that ice caps in the **polar regions** will melt,
25 causing oceans to rise. Many islands will disappear under the water and coastal areas will be flooded. Studies estimate that 35 percent of Bangladesh will be under water by
30 the year 2100. Many plants, fish, and animals will be unable to survive the warmer temperatures. Some parts of the world will get less rain and **crops** will suffer. The **drought** situation
35 is terrible in Africa, where more and more land becomes **desert** every year.

5 In 1997, Canada, along with another 160 countries, met in
40 Kyoto, Japan, to discuss how to

Oil fires can cause a great deal of pollution.

City of Edmonton Archives/EA-340-1311

Provincial Archives of Alberta, Photo P2882

© PEARSON LONGMAN • REPRODUCTION PROHIBITED

reduce greenhouse gases around the world. The countries set targets for lower production of gases; the agreement to achieve these **targets** was called the Kyoto Protocol. The Kyoto Protocol was signed by Canada in 2002. However, Canada did not meet its targets.

6   45 In 2009, leaders from over 190 countries signed the Copenhagen accord. The accord is designed to lower greenhouse gasses and slow down global warming. The accord is only an agreement, not a legally binding document.

7   It will be difficult for developing countries to improve their social and economic situation and, at the same time, meet climate change targets. The developed countries 50 have agreed to help financially.

8   For Canada, a big challenge is the oil sands of Alberta. The cost of extracting oil from these sands is expensive both in terms of money and the impact on the environment. Oil production from tar sands causes air and water pollution and is a major contributor to greenhouse gas emissions. Furthermore, many forests are destroyed to reach the tar 55 sands below. The Alberta government has pledged to capture the carbon dioxide in order to prevent its contribution to global warming. All countries contribute to global warming but some environmentalists say that Canada is one of the worst **offenders**.

COMPREHENSION AND DISCUSSION QUESTIONS

1. What causes global warming?

2. What are some negative aspects of global warming?

3. Do you think that the greenhouse effect will change Canada?

4. What do you think could slow down global warming?

5. What does carbon footprint mean?

LANGUAGE AND CONTACT ACTIVITIES

1. Writing an Article about Deforestation

Read the following information about deforestation. In point form, put the information from the reading into the outline that follows.

DEFORESTATION – INFORMATION
What is it?
The destruction or cutting down of forests (trees)
Where is it happening?
Southeast Asia, Central and South America, West Africa, Canada
How does it happen?
Logging for timber, clearing for crops, cattle ranching, industrial and urban development

© PEARSON LONGMAN • REPRODUCTION PROHIBITED

DEFORESTATION – INFORMATION

What are the results of deforestation?
Extinction of plants and animals, global warming, soil erosion

What can be done?
Plant trees, contribute money to people who are saving the rainforest, stop logging companies from cutting trees, don't buy products made of tropical woods (e.g., teak, mahogany)

Outline

1. Deforestation of Tropical Rainforests

   a. Definition _____

   _____

   b. Location _____

2. Causes of Deforestation

   a. _____

   b. _____

   c. _____

3. Effects of Deforestation

   a. _____

   b. _____

   c. _____

4. Possible Solutions to the Problem

   a. _____

   b. _____

   c. _____

   d. _____

Using your outline, write four short paragraphs about deforestation. Be sure to write complete sentences. Give your article a title. Exchange your writing with someone else. Read your partner's article. Correct any errors.

2. Finding the Main Point

Match the headlines below to the four stories that follow.

  A) Alberta Wind Farm is Largest in Canada

  B) 100-Mille Diet: Can it Be Done in Your Community?

  C) Advances in Geothermal Technology are Promising

  D) Family Saves on Energy Bills by Installing Solar Panels

© PEARSON LONGMAN • REPRODUCTION PROHIBITED

HEADLINE: _____
Story 1

Roman and Maria Carzan are recent immigrants to Winnipeg, Manitoba. When they found a house that met their family's needs, they decided to install solar panels to cut down on energy costs throughout the long, cold Canadian winter.

HEADLINE: _____
Story 2

Just outside Fort McLeod, Alberta, is the largest wind farm in the country. Windmills produce **renewable** energy without harming the environment. More than 32 000 houses can be powered by the electricity generated by this wind farm.

HEADLINE: _____
Story 3

A family in Edmonton took on the challenge to eat locally for a year. They bought only food produced within 100 miles (160 kilometres) of their city. This means that they could not have coffee, citrus fruits, and many other foods typically found in grocery stores. They tried the 100-mile diet to help the environment.

HEADLINE: _____
Story 4

Until recently, it was very expensive to extract heat from the earth's core. However, advances in heat pump technology have made the use of geothermal heating possible for many new homeowners and businesses. Although the cost of installation is high, the operating costs and the costs to the environment are low.

Follow-up

• How difficult would it be for you to try the 100-mile diet in your community? What foods would you miss the most? Where does your diet come from?

• Cars are a major contributor to environmental problems. What are the best solutions for eliminating pollution from cars?

• Have you ever seen a wind farm, or a geo-thermally heated building?

• What can an individual do to help stop global warming?

Wind farm

© PEARSON LONGMAN • REPRODUCTION PROHIBITED

3. How Can You Make a Difference?

Several environmental problems are outlined in the following chart. Fill in the chart with actions you think individuals can take to reduce these problems.

PROBLEM	CONSEQUENCE	SOLUTION	INDIVIDUAL ACTION
Greenhouse Effect Carbon dioxide and other gases are released into the atmosphere where they trap heat from the sun's rays.	• global warming (floods, drought, loss of agricultural land and natural **habitats**)	• reduce gas emissions • use alternative sources of energy (e.g., solar power)	• use cars less • eat less meat • plant trees
Ozone Depletion The ozone layer, which protects earth from **ultraviolet rays**, is being destroyed by chemicals such as CFCs.	• rise in skin cancer, **cataracts**, and life-threatening diseases • destruction of crops	• eliminate production of ozone-depleting chemicals	
Acid Rain Air pollution causes acid rain.	• kills plants and animals • damages buildings • harmful to human health	• reduce air, water, and soil pollution	
Deforestation Trees are cut down for timber and agricultural land.	• soil **erosion** • **desertification** • contributes to the greenhouse effect	• stop cutting down trees • plant trees	
Water Pollution Oceans, rivers, and lakes are being polluted through sewage, dumping of industrial waste, oil spills, etc.	• **contaminates** drinking water • kills fish and plants	• stop polluting the water • impose severe **penalties** on companies that dump waste into water	
Garbage Tons of waste accumulate every year.	• **landfill sites pollute** soil • factories produce pollution by continually producing new items to replace those that are thrown away	• reduce consumption • recycle, reduce, reuse • **compost**	
Endangered Animals The natural habitats of many animals are being destroyed.	• many different species of animals are becoming extinct	• provide more protected areas • impose **bans** and severe penalties	

© PEARSON LONGMAN • REPRODUCTION PROHIBITED

4. How Green Are You?

Fill out the questionnaire below to find out how environmentally aware you are.

Strongly Agree **1**   Agree **2**   Don't Know **3**   Disagree **4**   Strongly Disagree **5**

1. Sometimes, if I'm in a hurry, I throw cans into the garbage instead of recycling.   1 2 3 4 5

2. It's okay to take an elevator when you are going one or two floors.   1 2 3 4 5

3. Given a choice, I would rather ride a bike than drive a car.   1 2 3 4 5

4. All garbage breaks down in twenty years.   1 2 3 4 5

5. Disposable diapers cost more than diapers from a diaper service.   1 2 3 4 5

6. Any kind of leftover food can go into a compost heap.   1 2 3 4 5

7. I never **litter**.   1 2 3 4 5

8. I have at least three **hazardous** cleaning products in my kitchen.   1 2 3 4 5

9. It doesn't matter how much water I use, because it all goes back into the ground anyway.   1 2 3 4 5

10. Whenever I get cold, I turn up the heat.   1 2 3 4 5

© PEARSON LONGMAN • REPRODUCTION PROHIBITED

Scoring

Questions 1, 2, 4, 6, 8, 9, 10

Strongly Agree: **1** point
Agree: **2** points
Don't Know: **3** points
Disagree: **4** points
Strongly Disagree: **5** points

Questions 3, 5, 7

Strongly Agree: **5** points
Agree: **4** points
Don't Know: **3** points
Disagree: **2** points
Strongly Disagree: **1** point

Your Score:

45-50 Congratulations, you are already green. Keep it up and the world will be a better place.

35-44 Very good. You're making changes in the right direction.

25-34 You need to increase your environmental awareness.

0-24 You really need some help understanding environmental issues.

PRE-READING II

PRE-READING II

- What is globalization?
- Can you think of a company that sells its product in every part of the world?
- Do you think Canada is run by big corporations rather than government?
- Have you ever participated in a protest?

READING II
Globalization

1   Nowadays we hear the term *globalization* more and more often. People understand it in different ways. Some people think of it as the spread of the same fashions, the same diseases, the same food, and the same TV shows across the world. This trend is called *homogenization*. Other people see globalization as the takeover of the power invested
5   in elected governments by multinational corporations. In other words, big companies have more control over world events and economics than do individual countries. Still other people see globalization as a positive thing; they argue that the spread of a free market economy will raise the general standard of living for all people, create greater access to information and consumer goods, and improve access to health care and
10 literacy development.

2   In some ways, globalization is not new. England, for example, sent explorers to several places around the world to establish colonies. The people already living in these places were **exploited** and many lost their freedom and cultural heritage. The difference between England's colonization and multinational corporations' globalization today is
15 a matter of speed. New technology allows companies to spread information, political influence, and goods very quickly to all corners of the world.

3   The effect of globalization was felt strongly in 2008, when a downturn in the American economy caused problems for the whole world. There was very little government regulation of American banks, who lent money to people who wanted to buy new
20 houses. Many people borrowed money at a low rate to cover their mortgages, but the banks then increased the interest rates to a point where people could not afford to keep their homes. Even though Canada's banks were better regulated, Canada still felt the effects of the economic recession because of our close business ties with the USA. This recession led to a loss of jobs, dropping stock prices, and the closure
25 of many companies.

© PEARSON LONGMAN • REPRODUCTION PROHIBITED

COMPREHENSION AND DISCUSSION QUESTIONS

- Are there any positive aspects to globalization?

- Why are some people against globalization?

- Do you think the Canadian and the U.S. governments have the same viewpoint on globalization? Why or why not?

- Can you give examples of how the world is becoming homogeneous?

- How is your first country affected by globalization?

LANGUAGE AND CONTACT ACTIVITIES

1. Globalization Interview

In pairs, make a list of five questions about globalization. Together, find two people from another class and interview them, asking your five questions.

2. Abbreviations

Using the Internet, find the full names for the following organizations and describe their main purpose.

OAS	NATO
OECD	IMF
WB	OPEC
G8	FTAA
G20	WTO

3. Diseases

One of the results of globalization is the spread of disease. Thirty years ago, Canadians thought the outlook for health around the world was a very good one. With the development of antibiotics and vaccines, many diseases were eliminated. Today the picture doesn't look so good. Many bacteria and viruses have become resistant to drugs. In addition, new diseases have emerged. One of the worst of these is AIDS, which at this time has no cure. Using the Internet, find out about the following diseases: SARS, H1N1, avian flu (bird flu), West Nile virus, smallpox, malaria, ebola, cholera, typhoid, yellow fever, hepatitis, and dengue fever. Which of these can you catch in Canada?

© PEARSON LONGMAN • REPRODUCTION PROHIBITED

GLOSSARY OF TERMS

NOUNS

ban
an order that forbids something from being done

cataract
a film on the eye that can cause blindness

chlorofluorocarbon (CFC)
a gas containing carbon, hydrogen, chlorine, and fluorine; used to refrigerate goods and as an aerosol propellant

crops
plants grown for food

desert
a dry place where little vegetation grows

desertification
becoming a desert

drought
continuous dry weather

erosion
the gradual wearing away of rock or soil

extinction
becoming extinct, no longer in existence

fertilizer
chemical used to help plants grow

greenhouse
a glass building that traps the heat from the sun to help plants grow

habitat
natural home of a plant or animal

industrialized nations
Europe, North America, Australia, and Japan

landfill site
dump, place where garbage is stored

offender
culprit

penalty
a punishment such as a fine for failing to fulfill the terms of an agreement

polar regions
areas around the North and South Poles

racial profiling
a kind of discrimination based on racial background, ancestry, or religion

target
goal, objective

ultraviolet rays
dangerous, cancer-causing rays of the sun

VERBS

to ban
to stop, to prohibit

to compost
to convert organic matter to compost

to contaminate
to make dirty

to destroy
to ruin, to defeat

to exploit
to take unfair advantage of

to litter
to make a place messy or dirty, to leave trash behind

to pollute
to cause harm to the environment usually by introducing waste, chemicals, or toxins

ADJECTIVES

endangered
threatened with extinction

giant
very large, huge

hazardous
dangerous

renewable
not likely to run out

significant
important

© PEARSON LONGMAN • REPRODUCTION PROHIBITED

Test Yourself

Canada in a Global World

MULTIPLE CHOICE

Circle the best answer.

1. Which of the following is *not* a cause of global warming?
   A) deforestation   C) planting trees
   B) burning of fossil fuels   D) use of fertilizers

2. Which of the following is *not* a consequence of global warming?
   A) drought   C) flooding
   B) death of plants and animals   D) increase in world population

3. The _____ Protocol of 2009 is an agreement to reduce greenhouse gases.
   A) Copenhagen   C) Greenhouse
   B) Japan   D) Tokyo

4. CFCs are found in _____.
   A) refrigerators   C) dishwashers
   B) microwave ovens   D) washing machines

SHORT ANSWER

Answer the following questions.

1. What causes the greenhouse effect?

   _____

2. List two consequences of acid rain.

   _____

3. What are the results of deforestation?

   _____

4. List two consequences of ozone depletion.

   _____

5. Many Canadians believe in saving the environment. What do the three R's stand for?

   _____

6. List two positive aspects of globalization.

   _____

7. List two negative aspects of globalization.

   _____

© PEARSON LONGMAN • REPRODUCTION PROHIBITED

Chapter 9

How Is Canada Governed?

© PEARSON LONGMAN • REPRODUCTION PROHIBITED

MATERIALS REQUIRED: List of local MPs, MLAs, and councillors; pictures of politicians.

SKILLS EMPHASIZED: Reading comprehension; discussion; matching; expressing opinions; evaluating; organizing; letter writing.

TO THE TEACHER: Review language for sequencing (*first, after, now*), for arguing (e.g., *I don't see it that way, I don't agree, in my opinion*) and for summarizing a point (e.g., *in short, to conclude, in a nutshell*).

SUGGESTED GRAMMATICAL FOCUS POINTS:
Reading I: passive voice (e.g., *are called, was elected, was chosen, is represented*).
Reading II: type II conditional (e.g., *If I were the Prime Minister, I would …*).

PRE-READING I

- What do you know about the federal government?

- Who is the Prime Minister of Canada?

- What is the name of the party in power?

- Do you know who your own Member of Parliament (MP) is?

- How do people become Members of Parliament?

- Who is the Lieutenant Governor in your province?

- Who is the Premier of your province?

- Who is your mayor?

READING I
The Structure of Government

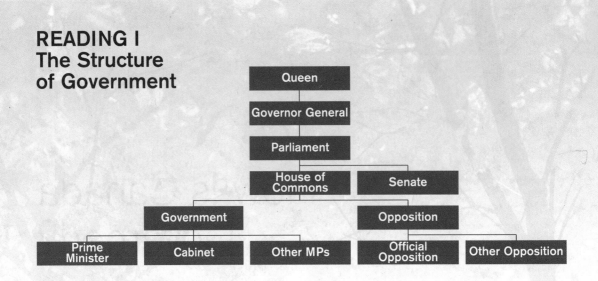

```
                    ┌─────────────┐
                    │    Queen    │
                    └─────────────┘
                           │
                  ┌──────────────────┐
                  │ Governor General │
                  └──────────────────┘
                           │
                    ┌─────────────┐
                    │ Parliament  │
                    └─────────────┘
                           │
            ┌──────────────┴──────────────┐
      ┌───────────┐                  ┌───────────┐
      │ House of  │                  │  Senate   │
      │ Commons   │                  │           │
      └───────────┘                  └───────────┘
            │                              │
      ┌───────────┐                  ┌───────────┐
      │Government │                  │Opposition │
      └───────────┘                  └───────────┘
```

| Prime Minister | Cabinet | Other MPs | Official Opposition | Other Opposition |

The Federal Government

1   The federal government is called Parliament. Parliament consists of the Crown (Queen or King), the House of Commons, and the Senate. Today Queen Elizabeth II is the head of Canada. Because she lives in England, she has a **representative** in Canada who performs her duties. Her representative is called the Governor General.
5   The people in the House of Commons are elected by the people of Canada. They are called Members of Parliament (MPs). The people in the Senate are chosen (appointed) by the Prime Minister. They are called Senators.

2   Members of Parliament in the House of Commons represent the people who elected them. Each MP usually belongs to a political party. After an election, the party that has
10   the most MPs forms the government. The leader of that party is the Prime Minister. The party with the second-most MPs elected forms the Official Opposition. Their leader is the Leader of the Opposition. MPs from other parties are also opposition members.

3   The Prime Minister chooses MPs (and sometimes Senators) to give
15   advice and help. These people are called Cabinet Ministers. The Cabinet Ministers have special jobs. For example, the Minister of Finance takes care of the government's money.
20   There are many people who work for the Cabinet Ministers. They are a part of the civil service. The people who work in the civil service are not elected. They apply for jobs with the
25   government in the same way that people apply for jobs with businesses.

Queen Elizabeth and Prince Philip. Queen Elizabeth is the head of Canada. She is represented by the Governor General of Canada and the Lieutenant Governor.

© PEARSON LONGMAN • REPRODUCTION PROHIBITED

© Rex Features/Ponopresse

Provincial Governments

4   Provincial governments are very similar to the federal government, except that the provinces have no Senates. The Crown is represented by a Lieutenant Governor. Each province has a legislative assembly that is similar to the federal House of
30 Commons. The Members of the Legislative Assembly (MLAs) or the Members of the Provincial Parliament (MPPs, as they are called in Ontario) and Members of the National Assembly (MNAs, in Quebec) are elected by the people in the province. Usually members belong to a political party. After an election, the leader of the party with the most elected representatives becomes the Premier of
35 the province. The leader of the party with the second-most votes becomes the Leader of the Opposition. The Premier of the province chooses Cabinet Ministers to look after provincial government departments: These are also called different things depending on the province.

Municipal Governments

5   People in cities and towns vote for a local or municipal government. Usually the
40 head of the municipal government is called the mayor and other members of this government are called council members or councillors. These people meet regularly to discuss local issues and make local laws (called *bylaws*).

© PEARSON LONGMAN • REPRODUCTION PROHIBITED

COMPREHENSION AND DISCUSSION QUESTIONS

1. Who is the official head of Canada's government?

2. Who represents the Queen in the federal government?

3. Parliament is made up of two parts. What are they?

4. What is the difference between them?

5. How is the Prime Minister chosen?

6. What do Cabinet Ministers do?

7. What is the civil service? Do you know anyone who works in the civil service? If yes, what does he or she do?

POLITICAL PARTIES

A political party is a group of people who share the same ideas about what the government should do. There are several political parties in Canada (the Liberal Party, the Conservative Party of Canada, the New Democratic Party, the Bloc Québécois, the Communist Party of Canada, the Green Party, etc.). Each party has a leader. The leader of the party with the largest number of elected MPs is the Prime Minister. The MPs who do not belong to a party are called Independents.

LANGUAGE AND CONTACT ACTIVITIES

1. Federal Government Matching Exercise

Match the words on the left with the definitions on the right. The first one has been done for you.

1. Governor General   __10__ one of the parts of Parliament

2. Prime Minister   ____ an appointed government official

3. Senator   ____ a group of MPs with special responsibilities

4. Federal government   ____ the Queen's representative

5. MP   ____ leader of party with the most MPs

6. Official Opposition   ____ an elected government official

7. Queen   ____ Government of Canada

8. Political party   ____ head of Canada

9. Cabinet   ____ party with the second-largest number of MPs

10. House of Commons   ____ group of people who share ideas about how to run the country

2. Find Out Who Is in the Government

Find the answers to the following questions by going to the Government of Canada website at http://canada.gc.ca.

• Who is the Governor General of Canada?

• Who is the leader of the Official Opposition?

• Which political party does that person belong to?

• Who is your MP?

• What party does he or she belong to?

• Who is your MLA, MPP, or MNA?

• What party does he or she belong to?

• Who is the mayor of your town?

From the Government of Canada website, find the list of people who have served as Canadian Prime Ministers since 1867. Who served the longest? Who served the shortest amount of time? Who served more than once?

3. Develop a Chart of the Provincial Government

Look at the chart of the federal government at the beginning of Reading I. Using the information in Reading I, draw a similar chart for the provincial government.

© PEARSON LONGMAN • REPRODUCTION PROHIBITED

4. The Queen

Queen Elizabeth II is the Head of State and Queen of Canada. In 2002, she celebrated her golden jubilee. In other words, it was her fiftieth anniversary on the throne. She visited Canada in October, 2002. The Queen also visited Canada in 2005 to celebrate Alberta and Saskatchewan's provincial centennials. Although many Canadians were happy to see her, some said that Canada does not need a queen. Do you think that Canada needs a queen? Do you think that Canada should appoint a Head of State from within the country? Explain your answers.

PRE-READING II

• How are laws made in your country of origin?

• Do you know how laws are made in Canada?

• Who makes the laws in Canada?

Passing a Law in the Federal Government

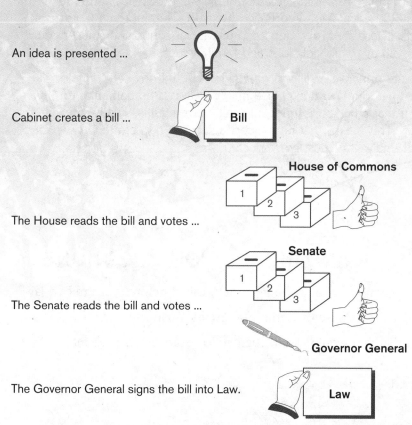

An idea is presented ...

Cabinet creates a bill ...

The House reads the bill and votes ...

The Senate reads the bill and votes ...

The Governor General signs the bill into Law.

© PEARSON LONGMAN • REPRODUCTION PROHIBITED

READING II
The Law and Canada's Justice System

1   In Canada, all federal laws are made in Parliament. Any MP or Senator can suggest a new law. First the MP or Senator writes an idea down on paper—this is called preparing a bill. All the MPs read the bill three times and talk about it. After the third reading, they vote *Yes* or *No*. The bill is also read three times in the Senate. If a majority of MPs and
5   Senators vote *Yes* for the bill, the Governor General signs the bill. This is called royal assent. The bill is then a law or an Act of Parliament.

2   In provincial governments, the procedure is similar, except there is no Senate. After a bill has gone through three readings in the Legislature, the politicians vote on the proposal. If the vote passes, the Lieutenant Governor signs the bill and it becomes a law.

3   10   Canada is a nation governed by law. Laws are written rules used to govern society, to provide order, and to express Canadian values. Everyone in Canada must follow Canadian laws. The justice system is made up of the government (who make the laws), the police (who provide safety and enforce the laws), and the courts (who resolve differences).

4   15   There are many different police forces in Canada (municipal, provincial, and federal); the best known is the Royal Canadian Mounted Police (RCMP). The Supreme Court is the highest court in Canada. There are also federal and provincial courts and smaller courts that deal with matters such as traffic violations and family issues.

5   Canadian law respects the principle of *habeas corpus*. That is, nobody can be held,
20   detained, or imprisoned without lawful explanation. As well, it is fundamental to the Canadian justice system that a person is innocent until proven guilty. The justice system is based on due process. This means that if a person is accused of a crime, he/she must be treated fairly and all legal rights must be respected.

© PEARSON LONGMAN • REPRODUCTION PROHIBITED

COMPREHENSION AND DISCUSSION QUESTIONS

1. Who can suggest a new law? What is the suggestion called before it becomes a law?

2. How many times does the House of Commons discuss a bill?

3. Are there any laws that you would like to change (for example, laws about immigration)?

4. What do the courts do?

5. What is due process?

LANGUAGE AND CONTACT ACTIVITIES

1. Choose a Side on a Canadian Issue

There are a number of **controversial issues** in Canada today. Some people would like to see changes in the laws that relate to **capital punishment, abortion**, and **the right to die**. Choose one of these issues. Using the Internet, find out what the law says about the issue you have chosen. Divide the class into two groups—one in favour of the issue, the other against. For example, one group will take the view that capital punishment should be **reinstated** while the other group will argue that there is no need for capital punishment. Work together to plan your arguments. Try to use information from the newspaper to support your arguments. Then debate your points.

2. Field Trip

Plan a trip to see the government at work. If you live in a capital city, phone your legislature to arrange for a tour. If you don't live in a capital city, phone your municipal government and arrange for a tour of city hall.

3. Group Discussion

In groups, discuss the following questions:
• Do you think the federal government is doing a good job? Why or why not?
• What do you think Canada's biggest problem is?
• What would you do if you were the Prime Minister?
• What do you think the biggest problem is in your province or territory?
• What would you do if you were the Premier?
• What do you think the biggest problem in your city or town is?
• What would you do if you were mayor?
• If you had a legal problem, where would you look for help?

4. Write to a Politician

As a class, choose an issue about which you would like to see a change in the law. The issue may be taxes, immigration, health care, abortion, or something else. Then, in pairs, discuss what you would like the government to do about this issue. Write a letter to a politician in the level of government (an MP, MLA, MPP, MNA, or Councillor) responsible for that issue. Use the following guidelines to write your letter:
• Clearly say what the issue is.
• Clearly say how and why you would like to see this law changed.
• Ask for a reply.
• Keep your letter short.
• Be polite.

© PEARSON LONGMAN • REPRODUCTION PROHIBITED

Canadian Issue

Taxes in Canada

Canadians sometimes feel that they are the most taxed nation in the world. Every year, people who have earned money pay income tax to both the federal and the provincial governments. People who own a house pay property taxes to the municipal government. Also, everyone pays an extra tax on purchases (GST, the abbreviation of Goods and Services Tax). When the GST was first introduced, the Canadian public protested very strongly, but the government started charging the GST anyway. In addition to the GST, all provinces except Alberta have a provincial sales tax (PST) on most items. Some provinces have combined the PST and GST into a harmonized sales tax (HST). These are all taxes that people are aware that they are paying. There are also hidden taxes, such as the taxes on cigarettes, gas, and alcohol. Traditionally, taxes were created to pay for services such as health care, employment insurance, Canada Pension, education, welfare, the upkeep of roads, and so on. Many Canadians feel that while governments are cutting back on the services, taxes keep going up.

Follow-up

When an ESL class was asked what surprised them most about Canada, several people said that they were shocked at how high the taxes are here. Interview a classmate and ask the following questions.

• Do you think taxes are too high?

• Do you think the government wastes money?

• Would you be willing to pay higher taxes for more services?

• In which areas do you think government should spend the most money: defence, scientific research, transportation, health care, education, or another choice?

• If the governments were to cut taxes further, which services could you live without?

• Are there any government services in Canada that are important to you that you did not have in your country of origin?

• Do you think too many or too few services are provided by the federal and provincial governments? Explain your answer.

© PEARSON LONGMAN • REPRODUCTION PROHIBITED

GLOSSARY OF TERMS

NOUNS

abortion
the termination or ending of a pregnancy

capital punishment
punishment by death for a crime

controversial issue
an issue on which people have conflicting opinions and views

representative
a person who has been chosen to act in place of another

right to die
the right to choose to end one's own life

VERBS

to reinstate
to bring back a law

Test Yourself

How Is Canada Governed?

MULTIPLE CHOICE

Circle the best answer.

1. The federal government consists of the following:
   - A) MPs, Senators, councillors
   - B) Crown, Lieutenant Governor, House of Commons
   - C) Governor General, MPs, Senators
   - D) Prime Minister, Cabinet Ministers, MLAs /MPP/MNAs

2. The Prime Minister appoints _____.
   - A) MPs
   - B) Cabinet Ministers
   - C) the civil service
   - D) Premiers

3. Royal assent occurs when _____.
   - A) the Governor General signs a bill
   - B) the mayor signs a bill
   - C) the bill is sent to the Senate
   - D) the Prime Minister signs a bill

4. The Governor General is the Queen's representative for the _____ government.
   - A) federal
   - B) provincial
   - C) municipal
   - D) all of the above

5. The Lieutenant Governor is the Queen's representative for the _____ government.
   - A) federal
   - B) provincial
   - C) municipal
   - D) all of the above

© PEARSON LONGMAN • REPRODUCTION PROHIBITED

6. The House of Commons reads a bill _____ time(s).

   A) zero   C) two

   B) one   D) three

7. The three levels of government in Canada are the _____.

   A) federal, provincial, national   C) local, provincial, municipal

   B) federal, Senate, civil service   D) federal, provincial, municipal

8. The official head of Canada's government is the _____.

   A) Prime Minister   C) Queen

   B) Cabinet Minister   D) Lieutenant Governor

9. The Prime Minister of Canada is _____.

   A) the person who gets   C) the leader of the party with
      the most votes   the most elected MPs

   B) the leader of the party   D) appointed by the House
      that gets the most votes   of Commons

10. The federal Parliament is made up of the _____.

    A) House of Commons, Senate   C) Government, Official Opposition

    B) Governor General, Prime Minister   D) Prime Minister, Cabinet

11. The provincial government is made up of _____.

    A) the Prime Minister   C) Cabinet Ministers

    B) MLAs/MPPs/MNAs   D) Councillors

TRUE / FALSE

Circle *T* if the statement is true. Circle *F* if it is false.

1. The people in the House of Commons are not elected. T / F

2. The people in the Senate are not elected by the people of Canada. T / F

3. People who work in the civil service are elected. T / F

4. Provincial governments have a Senate. T / F

5. The Queen is represented in the municipal government. T / F

6. Only a Member of Parliament can introduce a new law. T / F

7. The Governor General must sign a bill before it becomes law. T / F

8. The police can hold an individual without reason. T / F

9. The Supreme Court is the highest court in Canada. T / F

10. The RCMP are the only police force in Canada. T / F

© PEARSON LONGMAN • REPRODUCTION PROHIBITED

FILL IN THE BLANKS

In the blank, write in the word(s) needed to complete the sentence.

1. The present Prime Minister of Canada is _____.

2. There are _____ levels of government in Canada.

3. The people in the _____ are appointed by the Prime Minister.

4. The party that has the most MPs elected is the _____.

5. The party that has the second-most number of MPs elected is the _____.

6. The leader of the party with the most MPs elected is the _____.

7. The equivalent of the federal House of Commons in the provincial governments is the _____.

8. The leader of a provincial government is called the _____.

9. Municipal government is made up of the _____ and several _____.

10. When a new law is suggested and written down, it is called a _____.

11. _____ is when a bill is signed by the Governor General.

MATCHING

Match the following words with the appropriate definition.

A. Prime Minister

____ The Queen's representative in the provincial government

B. Governor General

____ Appointed by the Prime Minister

C. Lieutenant Governor

____ The leader of the party with the most MLAs elected

D. MLA/MPP/MNA

____ The leader of the party with the most MPs elected

E. Official Opposition

____ A person who is elected to the provincial government

F. Senator

____ The Queen's representative in the federal government

G. Premier

____ The party with the second most MPs or MLAs elected

H. MP

____ A person who is elected to the federal government

© PEARSON LONGMAN • REPRODUCTION PROHIBITED

SHORT ANSWER

Answer the following questions.

1. What is the role of the Governor General?

   _____

2. Who are the Members of Parliament?

   _____

3. How are Members of Parliament chosen?

   _____

4. How are Senators chosen?

   _____

5. How does Canada determine who will be Prime Minister?

   _____

6. What is the role of a Cabinet Minister?

   _____

7. What is the role of the Lieutenant Governor?

   _____

8. How does a person become the Premier of a province?

   _____

9. What is a *bill*?

   _____

10. What does *royal assent* mean?

    _____

11. What is due process?

    _____

12. What are the three components of the justice system?

    _____

13. Who is the MP in your area?

    _____

14. Who is the MLA/MPP/MNA in your area?

    _____

15. Who is the mayor of your community?

    _____

© PEARSON LONGMAN • REPRODUCTION PROHIBITED

Chapter 10 Elections

MATERIALS REQUIRED: Voter's kit, including sample ballots; pictures of campaigning; lawn signs.

SKILLS EMPHASIZED: Reading comprehension, discussion, sequencing, identifying, making choices, expressing opinions.

TO THE TEACHER: The Elections Canada website (http://www.elections.ca/) has numerous resources for teachers and students including crossword puzzles, quizzes, games, and information about all aspects of the electoral process.

SUGGESTED GRAMMATICAL FOCUS POINTS:

Reading: review passive voice, review a variety of verb tenses (simple present, present continuous, simple past, present perfect, etc.).

PRE-READING

- Have you ever voted before?

- Who can vote in your country of origin?

- Do you think you will vote in the next election in Canada?

- How do you decide whom to vote for?

- Would you like to be a politician?

- Do you know what a ballot is?

© PEARSON LONGMAN • REPRODUCTION PROHIBITED

READING
Elections

1   Canada is a representative democracy. This means that we **elect** people to make the
laws for us. At least every five years the Prime Minister calls an election for the federal
government and the Premiers call an election for the provinces and territories.
Municipal elections are usually held every three years. In a federal election, the country
5 is divided into approximately 310 sections (called ridings or constituencies). The
people who live in a riding vote for one person to represent them in the government as
a Member of Parliament (MP). In each riding, voters can choose among several
candidates who represent different political parties.

Before the Election

2   Once the Prime Minister has announced an election date, the people who can vote in
10 each riding are put on a voters' list. This is done to make sure that no one votes twice
and to make sure that only people who are **eligible** actually vote.

Who is Eligible to Vote in Canada?

3   • Canadian citizens who are over age 18.

• Citizens who have lived outside Canada for less than five years.

• Citizens outside Canada who work for the Canadian government.

4 15 At the beginning of an election period, a voter information card is sent to each person
on the voters' list. The card tells the voters where and when to vote.

5   Before voting, the people in a riding decide which **candidates**' ideas they like best.
They also decide which party they like best. Voters can find out what candidates think
by watching TV, reading the newspaper, going to party meetings, and reading **brochures**.

Election Day

6 20 On the day of the election, people go to a place in their neighbourhood called a *polling
station*, where they vote. When they arrive at the polling station, they give their names
to a poll clerk who checks to see that they are on the voters' list. The voters' names are
crossed off the list and they are each given a ballot. A ballot contains a list of the
candidates and their parties running in the election. An example of a typical ballot is
25 shown on the next page.

© PEARSON LONGMAN • REPRODUCTION PROHIBITED

7 Voters go to *polling booths*–
private places where they
can vote without anyone else
seeing the ballot. The voters
30 put a mark beside the name
of the person they want to
elect and then they fold the
ballot. Each ballot is then put
into a locked box. In Canada,
35 voting is by secret ballot. In
other words, voters don't
have to tell anyone whom
they voted for if they don't
want to. Also the poll clerks
40 never look at the ballots
when the voters put them in
the box. There are people
called scrutineers who make
sure that voting is done
45 properly.

Barbara Cheung New Democratic Party	○
Frank Bertinelli Liberal Party	○
Joe Johnson Green Party	○
Elaine Kearney Conservative Party	○
Marc Leduc Bloc Québécois	○

8 At 8:00 p.m. in every province, the polls close. The votes are then counted and the
Chief Electoral Officer announces the winners in each riding.

After the Federal Election

9 After the votes are counted
across Canada, the new
50 government is announced. Each
person who wins in a riding
becomes a Member of
Parliament (MP) and goes to
the House of Commons in
55 Ottawa. The party that has the
largest number of elected MPs
becomes the government. The
leader of that party becomes
the Prime Minister of Canada.
60 The party with the second-largest
number of elected MPs become
the Official Opposition. Other
parties with elected MPs are
also called opposition parties.
65 MPs usually fly or drive back
and forth between their ridings
and their offices in Ottawa.

Campaigning

© PEARSON LONGMAN • REPRODUCTION PROHIBITED

Provincial Archives of Alberta, Photo J697/1

COMPREHENSION AND DISCUSSION QUESTIONS

1. How often are federal, provincial, and municipal elections held?

2. What is a riding?

3. Who calls an election?

4. How do you get your name on a voters' list?

5. How can you decide whom to vote for?

6. Why is voting done by secret ballot?

7. After an election, how is the Prime Minister chosen?

8. Can you suggest a better system for running an election?

WHOM SHOULD YOU VOTE FOR?

Candidates who run in an election are usually nominated by the party they belong to. There are often several candidates from different parties running in the same riding. For example, in your riding there may be a Liberal, a Conservative, an NDP, and a Green Party candidate. Each candidate tries to get your vote by campaigning. This means that the candidate may come to your house to talk to you, appear on television and radio, express his or her views at community centres, and put signs up all over the riding. You may also get brochures about the candidate and the ideas of the party (called the *party platform*) in your mailbox. It is your responsibility to find out as much as you can about all of the candidates and the parties they represent in your riding. Then you can choose the candidate whose ideas you like the best.

LANGUAGE AND CONTACT ACTIVITIES

1. The Voting Process

Read the following steps involved in the voting process. Put them in the right order and number them from 1–9.

_____ The voter goes to a polling booth and votes.

_____ Voters go to the polling station to vote.

_____ Political parties start to campaign.

_____ The voter's name is crossed off the list and the voter is given a ballot.

_____ The votes are counted.

© PEARSON LONGMAN • REPRODUCTION PROHIBITED

____ The ballot is put into a locked box.

____ Eligible voters receive a voter information card in the mail.

____ The winners of the election are announced.

____ The Prime Minister calls an election.

2. Canadians' Concerns

Look in the *Letters to the Editor* section of your newspaper. What kinds of issues are people concerned about? Write some of these issues on the board. Choose one issue. What viewpoints do you and your classmates have on the issue?

3. Role Play an Election

As a class, choose two or more students to act as candidates who are running in an election. They have to take a side on one of the issues you have identified in the newspaper. They must try to convince the class to vote for them because of their views on the issue.

Make ballots using the names of the class candidates. Choose one person to be the poll clerk. The poll clerk can give the ballots to each person in the class. Now vote. Don't show your ballot to anyone else. Fold your ballot and give it back to the poll clerk. After everyone has voted, the poll clerk counts the votes. The candidate with the most votes wins.

4. Federal Ridings

Using the Internet, go to http://www.parl.gc.ca/

• Find out how many federal ridings there are in Canada.

• Which riding do you live in?

• Who is the MP in your riding? What political party is he or she affiliated with?

• For the following ridings fill out the chart below.

RIDING	MEMBER OF PARLIAMENT (MP)	POLITICAL PARTY
Edmonton Strathcona		
Cardigan, PEI		
Toronto Danforth		
Nunavut		

© PEARSON LONGMAN • REPRODUCTION PROHIBITED

Canadian Issue

Majority and Minority Governments

After the votes are counted, parties look to see who had the most elected MPs. If a party has the most MPs and also has more than half of all the MPs in the House of Commons, they form a majority government. This means that when there is a vote in the house, the government always has more people on its side than all the opposition members together. Sometimes, after an election, there are more MPs in opposition parties than in the government. In this case the government is called a minority government. Minority governments have a hard time passing laws because all the opposition members might vote against them. Also, the opposition parties can call for a vote of non-confidence. This means that all the MPs vote on whether the minority government should stay in power or a new election should be called.

Follow-up

• Find out how many seats each party in the House of Commons has today. Is there a minority or a majority government?

• Some democracies have only two political parties. With just two parties, there can never be a minority government. Do you think it is better to have many parties or to have only two parties? Explain your answer.

© PEARSON LONGMAN • REPRODUCTION PROHIBITED

GLOSSARY OF TERMS

NOUNS

brochure
a pamphlet that provides information

candidate
a person who runs in an election

eligible
fulfilling necessary conditions

VERBS

to elect
to choose by voting

Test Yourself

Elections

MULTIPLE CHOICE

Circle the best answer.

1. Federal elections must be held no further apart than every _____ years.
   A) 5   C) 2
   B) 3   D) 6

2. Who calls an election in Canada?
   A) the Prime Minister   C) the Queen
   B) the Governor General   D) the MPs

3. Canadians must be _____ years old in order to vote.
   A) 12   C) 18
   B) 16   D) 21

4. A majority government has _____.
   A) fewer seats than the official   C) more seats than all the other
      opposition   opposition parties combined
   B) the same number of seats
      as the opposition

5. All of the following are eligible to vote in Canada, except
   A) Canadian citizens under age 18.   C) Canadian citizens over age 18.
   B) citizens outside Canada who work D) citizens who have lived outside
      for the government.   Canada for less than five years.

6. Polling stations close _____
   A) at 8:00 p.m.   C) at 10:00 p.m.
   B) at 6:00 p.m.   D) whenever everyone on
                                    the voters' list has voted.

7. The candidate who wins the most votes in a federal riding becomes
   A) an MLA.   C) a Senator.
   B) an MP.   D) a Cabinet Minister.

8. The person who wins the most votes in a provincial riding becomes
   A) MLA/MPP/MNA.   C) a Senator.
   B) an MP.   D) a Cabinet Minister.

© PEARSON LONGMAN • REPRODUCTION PROHIBITED

9. Which of the following is an appointed position?

   A) MLA   C) Governor General

   B) MP   D) City Councillor

TRUE / FALSE

Circle *T* if the statement is true. Circle *F* if it is false.

1. The Prime Minister can call an election for a provincial government. T / F

2. Canadians under age 18 can vote in Canada. T / F

3. Canadians who work for the Canadian government outside of Canada can vote. T / F

4. Polling stations are only open until 6:00 p.m. T / F

5. A person must belong to a political party to become a Member of Parliament. T / F

6. Every Canadian citizen is eligible to vote. T / F

7. The person who becomes Prime Minister is the leader of the party with the most elected MPs. T / F

FILL IN THE BLANKS

In the blank, write the word(s) needed to complete the sentence.

1. The Prime Minister calls an election about every _____ years.

2. Municipal elections are called about every _____ years.

3. The place where Canadians vote is called a _____.

4. A _____ is a list of the candidates and the parties they represent for the riding.

5. Polling stations close at _____ p.m.

6. Federal elections are called by the _____.

7. A Member of Parliament who does not represent a party is called a(n) _____.

8. A _____ ensures that voting is done properly.

© PEARSON LONGMAN • REPRODUCTION PROHIBITED

ORDERING

The various steps in the election process are listed below. Number them in the order in which they occur.

_____ Eligible voters receive a voter information card in the mail.

_____ The voter goes to a polling booth and votes.

_____ The votes are counted.

_____ The ballot is put into a locked box.

_____ The winners of the election are announced.

_____ Voters go the polling station to vote.

_____ The voter's name is crossed off the list and the voter is given a ballot.

_____ The Prime Minister calls an election.

SHORT ANSWER

Answer the following questions.

1. What does representative democracy mean?

_____

2. What is a voters' list?

_____

3. What is a riding or a constituency?

_____

4. How can Canadian voters find out about the ideas of the different parties?

_____

5. What is the role of a poll clerk on election day?

_____

6. What does it mean when we say that voting in Canada is done by *secret ballot*?

_____

7. What is the role of scrutineers on election day?

_____

© PEARSON LONGMAN • REPRODUCTION PROHIBITED

8. How does someone become a Member of Parliament?

_____

9. Name four federal parties in Canada.

_____

© PEARSON LONGMAN • REPRODUCTION PROHIBITED

Chapter 11

Who Are These Canadians?

MATERIALS REQUIRED: *The Canadian Encyclopedia,* a camera.

SKILLS EMPHASIZED: Reading comprehension, discussion, identifying, surveying, comparing and contrasting, descriptive writing, role playing.

TO THE TEACHER: Supplement this unit by helping students find information about a local celebrity.

SUGGESTED GRAMMATICAL FOCUS POINTS:

Reading: review a variety of verb tenses, review *if … then …* statements.

© PEARSON LONGMAN • REPRODUCTION PROHIBITED

PRE-READING

• Have you ever heard of Terry Fox?

• Have you heard of the Marathon of Hope?

• Have you ever participated in a public run or walk?

READING
Terry Fox

1   Terry Fox was a young man from British
    Columbia who discovered he had cancer
    when he was eighteen years old.
    The doctors had to **amputate** one of his
5   legs. Terry wanted to do something for
    other people who had cancer. He planned
    to run all the way across Canada to raise
    money for cancer research. In 1980,
    he began the **Marathon** of Hope.
10 He started in St. John's, Newfoundland,
    and was headed for Victoria, BC. Terry ran
    an average of 42 kilometres a day for
    143 days. He had to stop near Thunder
    Bay, Ontario, when his cancer returned.
15 Terry died of lung cancer in 1981.

2   Terry Fox has become a hero to all
    Canadians for his **courage** and strength.
    Each year a Terry Fox run is held in most
    cities in Canada and in over fifty countries
20 worldwide to raise money for cancer
    research. People who enter the run each
    year get their friends and families to pay a
    certain amount of money for every kilometre
    they complete. This is called *sponsoring* a
25 runner. They try to get as many people as
    possible to sponsor the run.

Terry Fox

Gail Harvey, Photographer

© PEARSON LONGMAN • REPRODUCTION PROHIBITED

COMPREHENSION AND DISCUSSION QUESTIONS

1. Who was Terry Fox?

2. Why did he plan to run across Canada?

3. How far did he run before he had to stop?

4. Have you ever participated in a fundraising event?

5. Do you know where the marathon originated?

6. Why do you think that Canadians see Terry Fox as a hero?

Famous Canadians

Dr. Frederick Banting: Courtesy of New Tecumseth Public Library

Dr. Frederick Banting was a scientist. In 1922, he and Dr. Charles Best discovered insulin. Insulin is given to people with diabetes. Banting and Best's discovery has helped save the lives of people all over the world.

© Michel Ponomareff / Ponopresse

Oscar Peterson, born in Montreal, was one of the finest jazz pianists in the world.

John Kim Bell

John Kim Bell is a famous Native composer and conductor and a humanitarian. He created the National Aboriginal Achievement Awards in 1993.

Glenbow Archives NA-273-3

Emily Murphy was a popular writer from Alberta. She fought for women's rights in Canada. In 1929 Emily Murphy was responsible for having women declared as "persons" under the law.

Provincial Archives of Alberta, Photo B966

Pauline Johnson was a popular Métis author. She traveled across the country in the early 1900s to read her poetry. She wrote about the Mohawk culture.

© PEARSON LONGMAN • REPRODUCTION PROHIBITED

City of Edmonton Archives/EA-340-1758

Wayne Gretzky is also known as
"The Great One." He is considered by many
to be the finest hockey player of all time.

National Archives of Canada/ PA-114788

Dr. Norman Bethune was a Canadian surgeon who
helped the Spanish and Chinese during their civil wars.
Dr. Bethune is a hero to the Chinese people.

© Michel Ponomareff/Ponopresse

In 1984, **Madame Jeanne Sauvé** became the first woman
Governor General of Canada.

Julie Payette is the second Canadian woman
to have flown in space. Not only is Julie
an astronaut, but she is an accomplished
musician. She speaks Russian, German, Italian
and Spanish as well as being fluent in English
and French.

City of Edmonton Archives/ EA-499-93

Pierre Elliott Trudeau, Canada's most famous Prime Minister,
was a strong supporter of national unity and multiculturalism.
Under Trudeau's leadership, the Official Languages Act was
passed, making Canada officially bilingual. Trudeau also
brought the Constitution back to Canada and helped establish
the Charter of Rights and Freedoms.

© PEARSON LONGMAN • REPRODUCTION PROHIBITED

LANGUAGE AND CONTACT ACTIVITIES

1. Other Famous Canadians

Using a chart like the one below, ask five Canadians to name a famous Canadian in each of the categories listed:

ATHLETES	WRITERS	MUSICIANS	ARTISTS	SCIENTISTS	POLITICAL FIGURES	ACTORS

Once everyone in class has collected the names, compare your charts.

• Have you heard of any of these people before?

• Whose name appears most often in each of the categories?

• Why are these people famous?

• Were there any categories for which some people could not think of a famous Canadian?

2. Who Am I?

Choose one of the names on the chart. Find out as much as you can about this person by a) searching on the Internet, b) looking up the name in *The Canadian Encyclopedia,* c) asking your teacher, and/or d) asking other Canadians.

Take on the identity of the person you have chosen. Sit at the front of the class. Your classmates will ask you questions about your identity, such as "When were you born?" "Why are you famous?" and so on. They have to ask enough questions to guess who you are. They have three minutes to guess.

3. Name the Most Famous Person

Who is the most famous person in the world (living or dead) in each of the categories listed below:

cowboy	warrior	artist
engineer	humanitarian	royal person
movie star	religious figure	criminal
athlete	architect	doctor
political figure	singer or group of singers	scientist

© PEARSON LONGMAN • REPRODUCTION PROHIBITED

4. What do You Know About These Canadians?

In groups, go through the list and see how many of these names you recognize:

Donnacona	Tecumseh	Margaret Atwood	Leonard Cohen
Celine Dion	Anne Murray	Buffy Sainte-Marie	Diana Krall
Marshall McLuhan	Gilles Vigneault	Laura Secord	Joni Mitchell
Emily Carr	John Polanyi	Glenn Gould	J-A. Bombardier
Roberta Bondar	Pierre Berton	Nelly Furtado	A.Y. Jackson

5. Write a Biography About a Famous Person

Write a short **biography** about a famous person from your country of origin. Share it with the rest of the class. Be sure to include the following information:

- name
- sex
- when the person became famous
- why the person is famous

6. The Famous Five

Many women have fought for equal rights in Canada. Emily Murphy and four other Canadian women are known as "the Famous Five" because of their role in getting women recognized as persons in Canada. Under the Status of Women website (http://www.swc-cfc.gc.ca/), search for "the Famous Five" and find answers to the following questions:

- What was the Persons case?

- When was the Persons case?

- Who were the famous five? Where did they come from? What did they do?

- What contribution did each of the five women make to the Persons case?

- What other contributions did the famous five make to gain rights for women?

7. Canadian Honours, Awards, and Orders

There are several honours, awards, and orders given to Canadians for important achievements and contributions.

A) The Order of Canada is a major award given for outstanding achievement and service. It is administered by the Governor General and recognizes Canadians in all sectors of society. To find out about the Order of Canada, go to: http://www.gg.ca/ and answer the following questions:

- When was the Order of Canada set up?

© PEARSON LONGMAN • REPRODUCTION PROHIBITED

- Who created it?
- What is the award given for?

B) The Victoria Cross is the highest Canadian military honour and is awarded for bravery and courage in the face of an enemy. On the Internet, go the Veterans Affairs website (http://www.vac-acc.gc.ca/) to find answers to the following questions:

- Who was the first person to receive the Victoria Cross? When did he receive it? What did he receive it for?
- How many Canadians received a Victoria Cross after the Second World War?

C) The Nobel Prize is an annual international award administered in Sweden given for outstanding contributions to chemistry or physics or physiology and medicine or literature or economics or peace.

Lester B. Pearson (later to become Prime Minister of Canada) was awarded the Nobel Peace Prize in 1957 for his work in creating the United Nations Emergency Force (UNEF) which brought an end to the Suez crisis. The UNEF was recognized as the first UN peacekeeping force.

Over the years, several other Canadians have received a Nobel Prize. On the Internet, go to http://www.science.ca/scientists/nobellaureates.php and write a paragraph about a Canadian who has received the award. Make sure your profile includes answers to the following questions:

- Who won the award?
- What did he/she win the award for?
- When did he/she receive the award?

8. Autobiographies and Pictures

Write about yourself and your views of Canada. Be sure to answer the following questions:

- When did you come here?
- Why did you come?
- What do you like most about Canada?
- What do you like least?
- What makes Canada **unique**?

Take pictures of everyone in the class. Compile your stories and pictures into a book.

© PEARSON LONGMAN • REPRODUCTION PROHIBITED

GLOSSARY OF TERMS

NOUNS

athlete
a person who is good at sports

biography
the written story of another person's life

courage
bravery

marathon
a race over a very long distance

VERBS

to amputate
to cut off

ADJECTIVES

unique
unusual, special, one of a kind

Test Yourself

Who Are These Canadians?

MATCHING

Match the name on the left with the description on the right.

A. Terry Fox   _____ A famous Canadian hockey player

B. Emily Murphy   _____ Former Prime Minister of Canada

C. Dr. Frederick Banting   _____ The second Canadian woman in space

D. Jeanne Sauvé   _____ A young Canadian who wanted to raise money
for cancer research

E. Pauline Johnson   _____ A Métis author

F. Dr. Norman Bethune   _____ A writer who fought for women's rights in Canada

G. Julie Payette   _____ One of two scientists who discovered insulin

H. Wayne Gretzky   _____ The first woman Governor General

I. Pierre Elliot Trudeau   _____ A famous Canadian surgeon

SHORT ANSWER

Answer the following questions.

1. Who was Terry Fox?

_____

2. What is the Terry Fox run?

_____

3. Why was Emily Murphy important to Canadian history?

_____

4. Explain why Dr. Norman Bethune was famous.

_____

5. What did Dr. Frederick Banting and Dr. Charles Best discover?

_____

6. What is the Victoria Cross awarded for?

_____

© PEARSON LONGMAN • REPRODUCTION PROHIBITED

Chapter 12

What Is Typically Canadian?

© PEARSON LONGMAN • REPRODUCTION PROHIBITED

MATERIALS REQUIRED: A recipe for a Canadian dish.

SKILLS EMPHASIZED: Reading comprehension, discussion, interviewing, identifying paraphrases, comparing and contrasting, reading and giving instructions, expressing an opinion, predicting, reading a graph.

TO THE TEACHER: Cover vocabulary related to predicting events.

SUGGESTED GRAMMATICAL FOCUS POINTS:
Reading: review comparatives and superlatives, adjectives for describing people (e.g., *friendly, outgoing, cold*).

PRE-READING

- What did you know about Canada before you came?

- Have you spent a winter in Canada? If yes, how did you cope?

- Have you been to any national parks?

- What wildlife have you seen in Canada?

READING
A Portrait of Canada

1   The climate of Canada affects the people who live here. In many places, winter lasts up to six months. Although it can be mild in some parts of Canada, most people go through some **bone-chilling** weather each winter. The only way to enjoy the cold is to wear many layers of clothing, including **toques**, scarves, mitts, **parkas**, and winter
5   boots. The cold winters make many Canadians want to spend as much time as possible outside during the long hot summer days.

2   Canada is a huge country. Visitors are surprised at the long distances between cities. Even more surprising is the fact that Canadians will often travel hundreds of kilometres just for a weekend trip.

Mountain sheep

Herd of moose

3   10 Canada has many tourists every year. Many of them come to see the **wilderness**. Thousands visit the national parks and **wildlife** areas to see grizzly bears, moose, elk, deer, and mountain sheep. National and provincial parks are areas where hunting and development are strictly controlled. They are safe environments for plants and animals. The parks save nature for future generations of Canadians to enjoy.

4   15 Another important feature of Canada is that it is a bilingual country. In 1969, the Canadian government passed the Official Languages Act. This law says that all Canadians have the right to communicate with the federal government in either English or French. Every year there are more bilingual Canadians. Many schools have English or French language **immersion programs**.

5   20 Canada is a multicultural country. This means that Canada is made up of people from many different cultures. A main goal of multiculturalism is to treat all Canadians as different but equal. Canadians value people from everywhere. There are many social programs in Canada that are designed to make sure that everyone has access to education, health care, and shelter. Although Canada has some problems, in 2009,
25 the United Nations ranked Canada as one of the top five countries to live in. It is relatively safe and peaceful, and most people have a good standard of living.

© PEARSON LONGMAN • REPRODUCTION PROHIBITED

© PEARSON LONGMAN • REPRODUCTION PROHIBITED

Canada geese

Deer in the mountains

Watch out for grizzly bears like this one.

Beware of Bugs and Bears!

Although people love to spend time out-doors in the summer, they are sometimes driven inside by the bugs—black flies and mosquitoes especially. These biting **pests** can ruin a beautiful day unless you have lots of **insect repellent**.

People like to hike and camp in the wilderness but they have to beware of bears. There are bears in most parts of Canada. Bears can be very dangerous when people feed them or leave garbage behind. In the national parks, visitors are told how to keep food away from bears and what to do if they meet a bear.

COMPREHENSION AND DISCUSSION QUESTIONS

1. What does it mean to say that Canada is a bilingual country?

2. What does it mean to say that Canada is a multicultural country?

3. Were you surprised by the cold when you first came?

4. What sort of clothing do you wear in the winter?

5. Have you seen any wild animals in Canada?

6. How far would you travel for a weekend vacation?

Canadian Symbols

Canadian flag

The maple leaf has been a symbol of Canada for many years. It was adopted as the symbol for the Canadian flag in 1965.

The beaver: The beaver has been a symbol of Canada since the beginning of the fur trade. There is a beaver on the Canadian nickel (five-cent coin).

Fleur-de-Lys flag: The fleur-de-lys is a symbol of Quebec.

RCMP: For many tourists, the Royal Canadian Mounted Police (RCMP) are the major symbol of Canada. The police force began in the 1870s to keep peace in the west. The RCMP plays an important role today as Canada's national police force.

Parliament buildings from Chateau Laurier

© PEARSON LONGMAN • REPRODUCTION PROHIBITED

The Parliament Buildings in Ottawa

On November 11, Remembrance Day, many Canadians wear a poppy in memory of those Canadians who fought and died in wars.

Trade-mark of the Royal Canadian Legion - used under permission.

© Marcel Allard/Ponopresse

Loonies and toonies are Canadian one- and two-dollar coins. The dollar coin is called a loonie because the first time the coin was produced, it had a picture of a loon on one side. The loon is a bird that is found in most parts of Canada. Now, all dollar coins are called loonies, whether they have a picture of a loon on them or not. The toonie got its name because it rhymes with loonie and stands for two dollars.

British Columbia Archives, Photo # D-02021

Aboriginal art: Canadian aboriginal art is prized all over the world.

B. Korda/National Archives of Canada/PA-145170

An Inuit artist in an art centre

Department of Canadian Heritage. Reproduced with the permission of the Minister of Public Works and Government Services Canada, 2003.

Canadian Coat of Arms: The coat of arms bears Canada's motto, *a mari usque ad mare,* which is Latin for "from sea to sea."

© PEARSON LONGMAN • REPRODUCTION PROHIBITED

HOCKEY

Hockey is Canada's national game. The first organized team was started at McGill University in Montreal in 1879. In 1917, the National Hockey League (NHL) was formed. Over the years, new teams have been added to the league but one thing has not changed. Even though many of the cities in the NHL are in the United States, most of the best players are Canadian. Every spring, Canadians watch hockey nearly every night to see who the best team in the NHL is. The winning team gets the Stanley Cup. Fans in the city where the winners live celebrate for days. Hockey players make a lot of money. Many children play hockey from an early age, hoping to join the NHL. Hockey has become a very popular sport throughout Europe and North America.

Hockey has also become popular with girls. In fact, in 2010, both the Canadian women's and men's teams won gold medals at the Olympic Winter Games in Vancouver, BC. Most Canadians are extremely proud of their hockey fame.

Ladies playing hockey in Banff, Alberta, nearly 100 years ago

Hockey is Canada's favourite sport.

LANGUAGE AND CONTACT ACTIVITIES

1. Eating Habits

Interview another classmate using the following questions; then write a profile of your classmate's eating habits and views.

• What is your favourite food?

• Have your eating habits changed since you came to Canada?

• Do you cook? What do you like to cook?

• What do you think about **vegetarianism**?

• Are you **allergic** to any foods?

• Are there any foods that you won't eat? If so, why not?

• What kind of food do you think is typically Canadian?

© PEARSON LONGMAN • REPRODUCTION PROHIBITED

2. Recipes

Saskatoons are berries found all over the prairies. They are similar to blueberries, but they are smaller. Here is a recipe for Saskatoon Berry Pie. Read it carefully. Some of the instructions are not necessary and others are very important. Your friend has asked you for a short and easy recipe. Cross out the unnecessary instructions.

SASKATOON BERRY PIE

Frozen pie shell

4 cups of fresh Saskatoon berries (you can substitute blueberries if you do not have Saskatoons)

1 cup of sugar

4 tablespoons flour

2 teaspoons cornstarch

1 1/2 tablespoons lemon juice

1/2 teaspoon cinnamon

1 tablespoon butter

Line a 9-inch pan with a pie shell or pie crust; that is, put the pie crust inside a 9-inch pie pan.

Clean the berries. Wash them carefully, making sure to get all little twigs off them. Don't bruise the berries.

Combine the sugar, flour, cornstarch, lemon juice, and cinnamon. Put all these ingredients in one bowl and stir them together.

Mix the contents of the bowl with the berries. Sprinkle these ingredients over the berries and stir them gently until they are well blended.

Pour the mixture into the pie crust.

Dot the berries with butter; that is, take little bits of butter and put them all over the top of the berries.

Let the pie sit for 15 minutes. Then cover the berries with a top crust. If you like you can use a fork to make a pretty pattern in the pastry, but it is not necessary.

Make sure the oven is at 450°. Bake the pie at 450° for 10 minutes. Lower the heat to 350°. Bake the pie for another 30 minutes or until the crust is brown.

Write down your favourite recipe. Share it with the class. Together, plan a pot-luck party, where everyone cooks a dish and brings it to share with everyone else.

Canadian Issue
Canadian Cuisine

Many immigrants to Canada think that all Canadians eat the kinds of food found at shopping malls and in food courts. In fact, most Canadians don't eat that kind of **cuisine** at home. The cooking styles in Canada have come from all over the world. There are restaurants that serve the specialties of dozens of different countries. Although there are few truly Canadian dishes, regions of Canada are well known for some of the food they produce. On the West Coast people enjoy seafood, particularly salmon and crab. The East Coast is known for its lobster and cod. Alberta is famous for its beef, and more and more people are eating buffalo. Prairie wheat makes the finest pasta and bread. The fruit from the Okanagan region of British Columbia and Southern Ontario is transported all over the rest of the

© PEARSON LONGMAN • REPRODUCTION PROHIBITED

country. Wonderful berries are grown nearly everywhere in Canada. Quebec maintains French cuisine, and specialties include tortière (a meat pie), soups, poutine, and maple syrup. Wild rice is a **delicacy** found in Manitoba and Ontario. In the North, lake fish such as trout and Arctic char are very popular.

Follow-up

• Using the Internet, go to Canada's National Art Centre (http://www.nac.ca) and click on the link to Le Café. Go through the menus listed there and find food that is Canadian. Make up a completely Canadian menu.

3. Your Impressions of Canada

List the first impressions you had of Canada.

• What surprised you the most?

• What did you like the most?

• What did you dislike the most?

• What do you like about living in Canada today?

• What do you dislike about living here?

Write a paragraph about your first impressions of Canada and describe how your impressions have changed.

4. Typical Symbols

Ask five Canadians to tell you what symbols they think are typically Canadian. Compare the answers you've collected with those of your classmates.

• Which symbols were mentioned most often?

• Were there any answers that surprised you?

• What are typical symbols from your original country?

5. Hours of Daylight in Windsor and Inuvik

Locate Windsor, Ontario on a map.

The line graph on the next page shows the average number of hours of daylight for each month of the year in Windsor. Look at the graph and answer the following questions.

© PEARSON LONGMAN • REPRODUCTION PROHIBITED

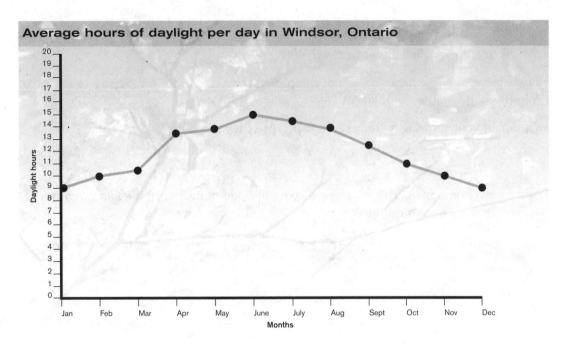

Average hours of daylight per day in Windsor, Ontario

• Which month had the most daylight?
• Which month had the least daylight?
• What was the average number of hours of daylight in December? In June? In September?
• What was the average number of hours of daylight for the whole year?

The graph below is called a bar graph. It shows exactly the same information as the line graph.

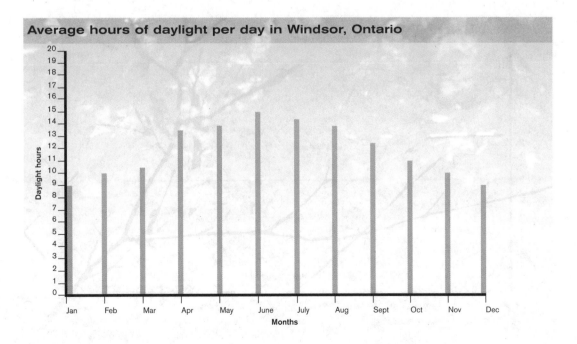

Average hours of daylight per day in Windsor, Ontario

© PEARSON LONGMAN • REPRODUCTION PROHIBITED

Compare the two graphs.

• Which one do you find easier to read? Why?

• Put a piece of blank paper on top of the bar graph. Make a dot on the top of each bar. Join the dots together with lines.

• Compare your drawing with the line graph. Are they the same?

Locate Inuvik on a map. The following are the average number of hours and minutes of daylight for each month in Inuvik:

MONTH	HOURS & MINUTES	MONTH	HOURS & MINUTES
January	3:08	July	22:01
February	7:41	August	17:35
March	11:41	September	13:15
April	16:16	October	9:10
May	21:05	November	3:50
June	24:00	December	00:21

Put the average number of daylight hours for each month in Inuvik on the graph below. Then make a line or bar graph.

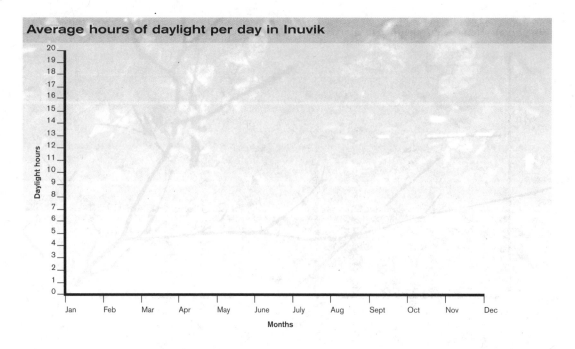

© PEARSON LONGMAN • REPRODUCTION PROHIBITED

- Which month had the most daylight?

- Which month had the least daylight?

- What was the average number of hours of daylight in December? In June? In September?

- What was the average number of hours of daylight for the whole year?

Compare the graph of Inuvik to the graph of Windsor.

- Are there any months that had nearly the same amount of daylight in both places?

- In Windsor, the number of hours of daylight ranges from a high of fifteen hours and fifteen minutes in June to a low of nine hours in December. What is the range in Inuvik?

- In which place would you rather live?

In Inuvik, there are fifty-five days in the summer that have twenty-four hours of sunlight. The sun never rises or sets on these days. In the winter there are thirty days when there is no sunlight at all. The sun neither rises nor sets. On how many days of the year in Inuvik does the sun rise and set?

Canadian Issue

Gun Control

Although there are many similarities between Canada and the United States, one **striking** difference is people's attitudes towards guns. While Americans protect their **right to bear arms**, most Canadians are proud to have strict gun control laws. In fact, some Canadians would like to ban all guns. The result of the gun control laws in Canada is that Canadians have much higher levels of personal safety. The number of deaths by guns in the United States is extremely high, while it is quite rare for Canadians to be shot to death.

Follow-up

- In pairs, write down as many arguments as you can in two columns: for and against gun control. Would you ever want to own a gun? Why or why not?

© PEARSON LONGMAN • REPRODUCTION PROHIBITED

Canadian Issue

The Canadian Identity: Is There One?

Every year around July 1st, newspaper and magazine columnists ask the question, "What does it mean to be a Canadian?" They never seem to come to a definite answer. Canadians have been described as friendly and cold, outgoing and **reserved, boring,** and **mysterious**. How is it that Canadians can be all these things at once? Canada is a nation of immigrants from all over the world. Every time a new group of people makes its home here, the country changes a little more. The beliefs and opinions of one group will often be very different from those of another.

Canadians think peace is important, so they usually try to **accommodate** each other. The way in which Canadians **adapt** to change is through compromise, or finding a middle ground. Some people see compromise, understanding, acceptance of differences, and a desire for peace as the **essential components** of the Canadian identity. Others say that these attributes only suggest that Canadians do not share a common set of values and that there is no Canadian identity.

Follow-up

• What is your impression of Canadian people?

• How would you describe the Canadian identity?

• How do you deal with people who have different beliefs and values from your own?

• Some immigrants comment that Canadian children have too much freedom and that they are badly behaved. They say that there is a need for more discipline. What do you think?

• Some newcomers say that although Canadians smile and seem friendly, they don't really welcome immigrants. Some people say that they would prefer open discrimination to what they believe is polite discrimination in Canada. What do you think about this?

• What do you think the Canadian identity will be in twenty years?

© PEARSON LONGMAN • REPRODUCTION PROHIBITED

GLOSSARY OF TERMS

NOUNS

component
part

cuisine
cooking

delicacy
a rare and highly favoured food

immersion program
a method of teaching a second language by teaching content through the new language

insect repellent
chemical used to keep insects from biting

parka
winter jacket

pest
an annoying insect

right to bear arms
the right to carry guns

toques
knitted winter hats

vegetarianism
the practice of not eating meat

wilderness
an area of land with no development

wildlife
plants and animals in the wild

VERBS

to accommodate
to make room for; to adjust

to adapt
to adjust

ADJECTIVES

allergic
suffering from a reaction to a substance

bone-chilling
very cold

boring
not interesting

essential
necessary

mysterious
not easy to understand

reserved
hiding feelings

striking
noticeable

Test Yourself

What Is Typically Canadian?

TRUE / FALSE

Circle *T* if the statement is true. Circle *F* if it is false.

1. Canada has very long summers. T / F

2. Canada has very long winters. T / F

3. The maple leaf was adopted as the symbol for the Canadian flag in 1965. T / F

4. The beaver as a symbol of Canada originated from the fur trade. T / F

5. The fleur-de-lys is a symbol for the province of Nova Scotia. T / F

6. The poppy symbolizes Thanksgiving. T / F

© PEARSON LONGMAN • REPRODUCTION PROHIBITED

7. The days in winter are short. T / F

8. Jasper is a national park. T / F

9. Canada is a multicultural country   T / F

FILL IN THE BLANKS

In the blanks, write the word(s) needed to make the sentence complete.

1. The two official languages in Canada are _____ and _____.

2. The fleur-de-lys is a symbol for the province of _____.

3. The symbol used to commemorate Remembrance Day is the _____.

4. The _____ was adopted as the symbol for the Canadian flag in 1965.

5. _____ is the most popular sport in Canada.

MATCHING

Match the Canadian symbols on the left with the description on the right.

A. Maple Leaf   ____ *A mari usque ad mare*

B. Beaver   ____ Canada's national police force

C. Fleur-de-lys   ____ Symbol on the Canadian flag

D. Poppy   ____ Symbol on the nickel

E. RCMP   ____ Nickname for the Canadian dollar

F. Parliament Buildings ____ Symbol on the Quebec flag

G. Loonie ·   ____ Symbol of Remembrance Day

H. Motto on the Coat of Arms ____ Located in Ottawa

SHORT ANSWER

Answer the following questions.

1. What is a national park?

_____

2. What does it mean when people refer to Canada as a bilingual country?

_____

3. What does it mean when people refer to Canada as a multicultural country?

_____

4. Why do Canadians call their dollar coin a *loonie*?

_____

5. What is a goal of multiculturalism?

_____

© PEARSON LONGMAN • REPRODUCTION PROHIBITED

© PEARSON LONGMAN • REPRODUCTION PROHIBITED

Chapter 13

Becoming a Canadian

MATERIALS REQUIRED: The Charter of Rights and Freedoms, sample citizenship application forms, *Discover Canada: The Rights and Responsibilities of Citizenship*.

SKILLS EMPHASIZED: Reading comprehension, discussion, comparing and contrasting, problem-solving, listing, letter writing, expressing opinions.

TO THE TEACHER: Supplement activities with exercises using the present and past perfect tenses. Obtain copies of citizenship application forms and *Discover Canada*. These are available on the Citizenship and Immigration Canada website (http://www.cic.gc.ca/) or through one of the Citizenship Call Centres.

SUGGESTED GRAMMATICAL FOCUS POINTS:
Reading I: conditional *would* (for problem-solving activity).
Reading II: review -*Wh* questions.

PRE-READING I

- Why do you think most people come to Canada?

- Have you heard of the Charter of Rights and Freedoms?

- What basic rights do you think all human beings should have?

READING I
Canadian Rights and Responsibilities

1 Many people come to Canada because they want to be free. Canadians have more freedom than people in many other countries in the world. The Charter of Rights and Freedoms is the law that gives Canadians their freedom. It is part of the Constitution, which is the most important law in Canada.

2 5 What kinds of freedoms do Canadians have?

• *Freedom of religion.* People can follow any religion. There are Christians, Jews, Muslims, Buddhists, Hindus, and people of other religions in Canada. There are also people who have no religion.

• *Freedom of thought, belief, opinion, and expression, including freedom of the press.*
10 This means that Canadians can say what they think and the news media can print stories that might not get printed in other countries. For example, if a Canadian doesn't like a politician, he or she is free to say so.

• *Freedom of peaceful assembly.* This means that a group of people can meet. In some countries, groups are not allowed to hold meetings.

3 15 Canadians also have basic rights:

• Canadians have the right to vote in elections.

• Canadians have the right to live and work anywhere in Canada.

• Canadians have the right to run in an election.

• Canadians have the right to be treated equally regardless of sex, race, colour, national
20 or ethnic origin, sexual orientation, age, mental or physical disability.

• Canadians have legal rights. They cannot be arrested without an explanation. Their property cannot be searched or taken away without explanation.

4 The following responsibilities go along with the rights:

• to vote in elections

25 • to be loyal to Canada

• to learn and to obey the laws of the country

• to **refrain** from discrimination against others

• to participate in the community

• to care for Canada's heritage

5 30 For Canada to function well as a society, it is important for all Canadians to take their rights and responsibilities seriously.

© PEARSON LONGMAN • REPRODUCTION PROHIBITED

COMPREHENSION AND DISCUSSION QUESTIONS

1. Name three freedoms that Canadians enjoy.

2. Name four rights.

3. Are there any rights that Canadians have that you didn't have in the country that you came from? Are there any rights that people in your former country have that Canadians don't have?

4. What do you think it means to be loyal to Canada?

5. Are there any laws in Canada that are different from the laws in your former country?

6. What are some ways in which you can participate in the community?

LANGUAGE AND CONTACT ACTIVITIES

1. Responsibilities of Canadian Citizens

List the responsibilities of Canadian citizens and give an example of each one. One example is given:

RESPONSIBILITY	EXAMPLE
Care for Canada's heritage	Don't litter

2. Problem-solving

In pairs or groups, discuss how you would handle the following situations involving rights and responsibilities:

• Your drunken neighbour makes loud noise all night long.

• Your child comes home from school and tells you that children were calling her **nasty** names.

• Your Chinese friend phones to see an apartment. As soon as the landlord sees that he is Chinese, he says the apartment has been rented. You find out later that the apartment hadn't been rented.

• You look out the window and see someone breaking into the house across the street.

• You are working a lot of overtime and you are not getting paid for it. Your boss says that he just can't afford to pay for your overtime.

Can you think of some difficult situations where people's rights have been **violated** or where other people have not met their responsibility?

© PEARSON LONGMAN • REPRODUCTION PROHIBITED

3. Volunteering

Use the Internet to find out if there is a central volunteer bureau in your community (http://volunteer.ca/). Phone, use the Internet, or write to the bureau for information on the types of volunteer jobs available. If there is no central volunteer bureau, contact the United Way and ask for someone to come to your class to talk about volunteer opportunities.

Provincial Archives of Alberta, Photo J3019

Canadians participate in many volunteer activities to raise money for different charities. These people are in a fun run.

Canadian Issue

The Role of Community

One of the responsibilities of Canadians is to participate in the community. Each group of immigrants faces difficult situations. Without the support of people in their communities, it would be even harder for newcomers. Today, participation in the community can mean many different things. Volunteers can partly address social problems. For example, every large city in Canada has food banks. People **donate** food and hours of work to help others who do not have enough food. Canadians volunteer to help at community celebrations, in ESL programs, and at hospitals, churches, and social service agencies. People also **coach** children in sports and help out at schools. There are many different ways to participate in a community.

Follow-up

• Do you do any volunteer work?

• Some people have criticized the existence of food banks. They say that the government has the responsibility to provide for the needs of disadvantaged people. They say that as long as food banks exist, the government will not meet its responsibility. What do you think?

• The federal government spends a lot of money providing language classes for newcomers. The purpose of this spending is to help immigrants become active participants in the Canadian community. Do you think these programs work? What do you think would be the best way to help immigrants participate in the community?

© PEARSON LONGMAN • REPRODUCTION PROHIBITED

PRE-READING I

PRE-READING II

• Do you know anyone who has recently become a Canadian citizen?

• Are you planning to become a Canadian citizen?

• What does it mean to be a Canadian?

• What steps do you have to go through to become a Canadian?

READING II
Applying for Canadian Citizenship

1 Chunhui and Ming Ming Cheung came to Canada four years ago with their two children, Sue (age six) and Victor (age nine). They started a small cleaning business in Toronto that is doing very well. Although the first year was difficult for the Cheungs, they **gradually** started to feel comfortable in Canada. When they had been here for
5 three years, they decided to become Canadian citizens.

2 Ming Ming phoned the Citizenship Call Centre in Toronto to find out what the Cheungs needed to do. She arranged to have some application forms mailed to them. When she received the forms (two for adults and two for her children), she made a list of all the **documents** they would need, she made photocopies of all the documents, and she
10 and Chunhui filled out the applications. They sent the applications, the copied documents, signed photographs, and payment for the application fees to an address in Sydney, Nova Scotia.

3 Shortly after they sent in their applications, the Cheungs received a letter acknowledging that their applications had been received. They were also sent a booklet *Discover Canada:*
15 *the Rights and Responsibilities of Citizenship*. The book covered all the information they would need to know to pass the Canadian Citizenship test. Topics included Canadian geography, history, government, elections, and rights and responsibilities. The Cheungs both studied hard for the test.

4 Finally Chunhui and Ming Ming were **notified** of the day and place of the test.
20 They were very nervous. They took the test. Both of them passed. Their studying was successful.

5 The last and most enjoyable step for the Cheungs was the citizenship **ceremony**. Everyone dressed up in his or her best clothes. When they got to the hall, the children were excited to see a **Mountie** in a red uniform. There were many other people getting
25 their citizenship too. First, there was a speech, and later citizenship was awarded to all the new Canadians. The Cheungs felt very proud as they repeated the **oath** of Canadian citizenship. Ming Ming had tears in her eyes. There was a **reception** after the ceremony. Then the whole family went out for dinner to celebrate their new country.

© PEARSON LONGMAN • REPRODUCTION PROHIBITED

COMPREHENSION AND DISCUSSION QUESTIONS

1. How many years were the Cheungs in Canada before they decided to become Canadian citizens?

2. What steps are involved in becoming a Canadian?

3. What do people have to know to pass the citizenship test?

4. Do you think it is important for Canadians to know about geography? History? Government? Elections? Rights and responsibilities? Explain your answers.

LANGUAGE AND CONTACT ACTIVITIES

1. The Citizenship Application Form

Get a citizenship application form from the Internet (http://www.cic.gc.ca/) or from one of the Citizenship Call Centres. Answer the following questions.

• What documents must be provided with your application?

• Can you use passport photos?

• Can you apply for more than one person on a single form?

• Which of the following information is not required?

  a) marital status

  b) birthdate

  c) date of entry to Canada

  d) place of work

• Why do you think the government wants to know whether an applicant has committed a crime? Do you think that someone who has committed a crime should be allowed to become a citizen?

2. The Citizenship Ceremony

Choose one student to phone the citizenship office in your community. The student should ask where and when the next citizenship ceremony will be held. Arrange as a class to go to the ceremony. After the ceremony, talk to some of the new Canadians. Ask them how they feel.

A Canadian citizenship ceremony

© PEARSON LONGMAN • REPRODUCTION PROHIBITED

© Raffi Kirdi / Ponopresse

The Oath of Citizenship

I swear (or affirm)
that I will be faithful
and bear true allegiance
to Her Majesty Queen Elizabeth the Second,
Her Heirs and Successors
and that I will faithfully observe
the laws of Canada
and fulfil my duties as a Canadian citizen.

GLOSSARY OF TERMS

NOUNS

ceremony
formal celebration

documents
legal papers

Mountie
Royal Canadian Mounted Police
(RCMP) officer

oath
sacred promise

reception
party, gathering

VERBS

to coach
to teach

to donate
to give

to notify
to tell

to refrain
to stop, to keep from doing something

to violate
to show disrespect

to volunteer
to give of one's time, to work for no
pay

ADJECTIVES

nasty
mean, cruel

ADVERBS

gradually
slowly

© PEARSON LONGMAN • REPRODUCTION PROHIBITED

Test Yourself

Becoming a Canadian

MULTIPLE CHOICE

Circle the best answer.

1. Which of the following is not a freedom of Canadians?
   A) the freedom to steal
   B) the freedom of religion
   C) the freedom of the press
   D) the freedom of assembly

2. Canadians have the basic right to _____.
   A) take Sundays off from work
   B) take the law into their own hands
   C) run in an election
   D) discriminate against others

3. Which of the following is not a basic right of Canadians?
   A) the right to run in an election
   B) the right to be treated equally
   C) the right to vote in elections
   D) the right to bear arms

4. Which of the following is not a responsibility of Canadians?
   A) to participate in the community
   B) to accept the government's decisions
   C) to vote in elections
   D) to be loyal to Canada

5. Along with their rights, Canadians are responsible to _____.
   A) make sure others follow the laws of Canada
   B) treat other cultural groups differently
   C) support political candidates even if they do not like them
   D) care for Canada's heritage

6. An example of voluntary work is _____.
   A) a job that pays equal to or less than minimum wage
   B) cleaning your house on the weekend
   C) donating your time and effort to a cause
   D) doing work you don't like

TRUE / FALSE

Circle *T* if the statement is true. Circle *F* if it is false.

1. Canadians have less freedom than people in most other countries. T / F

2. A Canadian does not have the right to express dissatisfaction with the government. T / F

3. Canadians have the freedom the follow any religion they wish. T / F

4. Canadians do not have the freedom to meet in groups. T / F

© PEARSON LONGMAN • REPRODUCTION PROHIBITED

5. Canadians have the right to vote in elections. T / F

6. Canadians are not free to live and work anywhere in Canada. T / F

7. Canadians should be loyal to Canada. T / F

FILL IN THE BLANKS

In the blank, write the word(s) needed to make the sentence complete.

1. Being able to go to any church or any temple is an example of

   _____.

2. Canadians have _____ freedom than people in many other countries.

3. Learning and obeying the laws of Canada are _____.

4. _____ is the law that ensures Canadians' freedom.

5. To be treated equally in Canada is a _____.

6. Teaching literacy classes on Saturday mornings without being paid is an example of _____.

SHORT ANSWER

Answer the following questions.

1. Identify three freedoms of Canadians.

   _____

2. Identify four basics rights of Canadians.

   _____

3. Identify five responsibilities of Canadians.

   _____

4. What does it mean when we say that Canadians have freedom of the press?

   _____

   _____

5. Why do you want to become a Canadian?

   _____

   _____

© PEARSON LONGMAN • REPRODUCTION PROHIBITED

Appendix I

Useful Website Resources

GENERAL INFORMATION ABOUT CANADA

Government of Canada Website: The Government of Canada's primary Internet site, this site provides general information about Canada and access to federal government departments, programs, and services.
http://canada.gc.ca/

Provinces and Territories Website: Provides links to each of the provincial and territorial websites.
http://canada.gc.ca/othergov-autregouv/prov-eng.html

The Canadian Encyclopedia: Online version of Canadian Encyclopedia sponsored by the Historica Foundation (a charitable foundation dedicated to promoting Canadian History Education).
http://www.thecanadianencyclopedia.com/

Statistics Canada: Gives data on Canada's economy, land, people and government as well as a variety of learning resources.
http://www.statcan.gc.ca/

Canadiana: The Canadian Resource Page: Provides a wealth of information on all aspects of Canada.
http://www.cs.cmu.edu/afs/cs.cmu.edu/Web/Unofficial/Canadiana/

Oh Canada: The All-Canadian Website: Provides access to numerous topics on Canada including government sites, sports, entertainment, business, and current topics.
http://www.iaw.on.ca/ohcanada/

The Parliament of Canada: Displays a large number of photos from the Parliament of Canada Photo Gallery and gives information about the parliamentary process (making laws, the function of the House of Commons and Senate, etc.).
http://www.parl.gc.ca

The Governor General of Canada
http://www.gg.ca/

© PEARSON LONGMAN • REPRODUCTION PROHIBITED

NATIVE PEOPLES

Aboriginal Multi-Media Society: Lists aboriginal media sites across the country, describes upcoming festivals and ceremonies, and provides links to educational resources and famous native Canadians.
http://www.ammsa.com/index.htm

Indian and Northern Affairs Canada: Government of Canada site that focuses on First Nations issues; this site provides links to sites concerned with policy, programs and services, current events and issues, and culture and history.
http://www.ainc-inac.gc.ca/

Native American Indian Resources: Over 300 web pages dealing with a variety of topics including stories by native authors, recipes, information about native artists, games, etc.
http://www.kstrom.net/isk/mainmenu.html

Aboriginal Canada Portal: Provides access to a wide variety of national, provincial, and local information about Aboriginal peoples of Canada.
http://www.aboriginalcanada.gc.ca

CITIZENSHIP AND IMMIGRATION

Citizenship and Immigration Canada: Information about Canada's immigration policy, becoming a citizen, and available programs and services. From this site, one can obtain citizenship application forms, the citizenship study guide (Discover Canada: The Rights and Responsibilities of Citizenship) and sample test questions.
http://www.cic.gc.ca/

CANADIAN HISTORY

The Historica-Dominion Institute: Independent organization dedicated to Canadian history, identity and citizenship. The website provides access to programs and projects on historical topics and current affairs.
http://www.historica-dominion.ca/en/

History by the Minute: Short films about Canada's past including topics such as sports, First Nations, exploration, Canadian heroes, women, and the military.
http://www.histori.ca/minutes/

Veteran Affairs
http://www.vac-acc.gc.ca/

MAPS, PICTURES, PHOTOGRAPHS, BIOGRAPHIES

Free Maps of Canada: Offers a large selection of maps of Canada and the provinces that can be downloaded for classroom use. The site includes blank maps and activities for creating maps.
http://geography.about.com/library/blank/blxcanada.htm

The National Atlas of Canada: Information about Canada through maps, facts, quizzes, and other resources.
http://atlas.gc.ca/site/index.html

© PEARSON LONGMAN • REPRODUCTION PROHIBITED

Famous Canadians: Photographs and biographical information about famous Canadians. This site also provides links to instructional materials that teachers can use to design lessons around the theme of famous Canadians.
http://www.cln.org/themes/famous.html

ELECTIONS

Elections Canada: Presents information about the federal electoral system, including the steps involved in all aspects of an election, reports of political parties and candidates, results of past elections, and so on.
http://www.elections.ca/

JUSTICE SYSTEM

Canada's System of Justice
http://www.justice.gc.ca/

ARTS AND CULTURE

Images Canada: Offers search access to thousands of images held on the websites of participating Canadian cultural institutions: images of Canadian events, people, places and things that make up Canada's collective heritage.
http://www.imagescanada.ca/

Canadian Heritage: Provides information about numerous aspects of Canadian culture, including Canadian symbols, music, books, holidays, sports, and multiculturalism.
http://www.pch.gc.ca/

Culture Canada: Offers access to information and government resources on the topics of culture, heritage, and recreation.
http://culturecanada.gc.ca

ENVIRONMENTAL ISSUES

Canadian Wildlife Service: Government of Canada website that provides information on issues related to wildlife, including protection and management of wildlife, environmental concerns, endangered species, etc.
http://www.cws-scf.ec.gc.ca/

Natural Resources Canada: Information about climate change and other environmental issues.
http://www.nrcan-rncan.gc.ca/

Parks Canada: Information about Canadian national parks and historic sites, trip-planning, learning resources, and volunteer opportunities. Also includes quizzes and games.
http://www.parkscanada.gc.ca/

Environment Canada: Government of Canada's Internet resource for weather and environmental information; includes information about what you can do.
http://www.ec.gc.ca/

© PEARSON LONGMAN • REPRODUCTION PROHIBITED

QUIZZES

Test Your Geography Knowledge: Online Canadian geography quiz.
http://www.lizardpoint.com/fun/geoquiz/canquiz.html

Geography and History Quizzes
http://atlas.nrcan.gc.ca/site/english/learningresources/quizzes/index.html

LIBRARIES, MUSEUMS, AND ARCHIVES

The National Arts Centre
http://www.nac-cna.ca/

The Internet Public Library
http://www.ipl.org/div/news/

National Archives and National Library of Canada
http://www.archives.ca/index.html

Canadian Museum of Civilization and Canadian War Museum
http://www.civilization.ca/

VOLUNTEERING

Volunteer Information and Opportunities
http://volunteer.ca/

Disclaimer: The URLs for some of these websites may change. The authors of *Being Canadian* are not responsible for the accuracy of the information contained on these websites.

© PEARSON LONGMAN • REPRODUCTION PROHIBITED

References and Photo Credits

REFERENCES

The Canadian Encyclopedia: Year 2000 Edition (1999). Toronto: McClelland & Stewart.

Forsey, E. A. (1997). *How Canadians Govern Themselves*. 4th Edition. Ottawa: Ministry of Supply and Services.

Government of Canada (1989). *Canada: A Portrait*. Ottawa: Ministry of Supply and Services.

McKie, C. & Thompson, K. (1990). *Canadian Social Trends*. Vols. 1 & 2. Toronto: Thompson Educational Publishing.

PHOTO CREDITS

Front cover photos (from left to right) BIGSTOCK; SHUTTERSTOCK/Metalstock; SHUTTERSTOCK/Demid; back cover photos (from left to right) BIGSTOCK; SHUTTERSTOCK/P. Binet; SHUTTERSTOCK/Deb22. Reproduced with permission; p. 7, Victoria: Dean Brandhagen; Banff: Canadian Tourism Commission/Commission canadienne du tourism; Calgary Stampede: Glenbow Archives NA-335-30; p. 8, Prairies: Provincial Archives of Alberta, Photo B2349; Quebec: Canadian Tourism Commission/Commission canadienne du tourism; p. 9, Nova Scotia: Canadian Tourism Commission/Commission canadienne du tourism; Prince Edward Island: Canadian Tourism Commission/Commission canadienne du tourism; Toronto: Tourism Toronto; Newfoundland: Canadian Tourism Commission/Commission canadienne du tourism; p. 10, Baffin Island: Ed Ticknor; p. 13, Driving in winter: Provincial archives of Alberta, Photo J3808/1; p. 18, Indians in BC: National Archives of Canada / C-011336; Totem poles: Glenbow archives NA-1700-56; p. 19, Buffalo herds: Glenbow Archives ND-8-247; Native tepee: A. Rafton-Canning / National Archives of Canada / C-024214; Inuit hunter: Canadian Tourism Commission/ Commission canadienne du tourism; Potlatches: British Columbia Archives, Photo #E-04017; p. 20, Inuit mother and child: Richard Harrington / National Archives of Canada / PA-145005; Innu in Labrador: Photograph attributed to Fred C. Sears / National Archives of Canada / PA-148593; p. 28, Indian chief: O.B. Buell / National Archives of Canada / PA-118768; p. 29, Fur trading: Richard Harrington / National Archives of Canada / PA-129942; p. 31, Hudson's Bay store: Glenbow Archives NA-622-2; p. 34, Caribbean community: TonyEno.com; p. 40, Sir John A. Macdonald: William James Topley / National Archives of Canada / PA-027013; Louis Riel: National Archives of Canada / PA-139073; p. 44, Constitution Act: Robert Cooper / National Archives of Canada / PA-141503; p. 52, Railway bridge: Alexander Henderson, National Archives of Canada / PA-164446; Canadian Pacific Railway: National Archives of Canada / C-021427; Lord Strathcona: British Columbia Archives, Photo #A-01744; p. 54, The Canadian National Vimy Memorial / Shutterstock; p. 56, Chinese work camp: Surveyor-General Édouard Deville / National Archives of Canada / C-016715; p. 58, Border traffic: www.TwoGypsies.com; p. 62, Homestead: J.A. Fletcher / National Archives of Canada / PA-017378; p. 63, Klondike gold rush: Glenbow Archives NA-912-9; p. 74, Farm in Manitoba: Canadian Tourism Commission/ Commission canadienne du tourism; p. 75, Log boom: Glenbow Archives NA-864-3; Oil production in Alberta: Provincial Archives of Alberta, Photo P1199; p. 81, Canadians enjoying summer: Caron Rollins; p. 82, Canadians enjoying winter: Provincial Archives of Alberta, Photo J3021; p. 84, Edmonton Folk Festival: Caron Rollins; p. 88, Power plant: City of Edmonton Archives / EA-340-1311; Oil fires: Provincial Archives of Alberta, Photo P2882; p. 91, Wind farm / Shutterstock; p. 100, Queen Elizabeth and Prince Philip: © Rex Features / Ponopresse; p. 113, Campaigning: Provincial Archives of Alberta, Photo J697/1; p. 122, Terry Fox: Gail Harvey; p. 123, Dr. Frederick Banting, Courtesy of New Tecumseh Public Library; Oscar Peterson: © Michel Ponomareff / Ponopresse; John Kim Bell: John Kim Bell; Emily Murphy: Glenbow Archives NA-273-3; Pauline Johnson: Provincial Archives of Alberta, Photo B966; p. 124, Wayne Gretzky: City of Edmonton Archives / EA -340-1758; Dr. Norman Bethune: National Archives of Canada / PA-114788; Jeanne Sauvé: © Michel Ponomareff / Ponopresse; Pierre Elliott Trudeau: City of Edmonton Archives/EA-499-93; p. 130, Sheep: Albert Van / National Archives of Canada / PA-126684; Moose: Glenbow Archives NA-424-11; p. 131, Geese: Glenbow Archives NA-4868-338; Bear: Glenbow Archives NA-3910-96; Deer: Glenbow Archives NA-4868-250; p. 132, Beaver: Glenbow Archives NA-2411-1; RCMP: British Columbia Archives, Photo #1-29225; Parliament: © Michel Ponomareff / Ponopresse; p. 133, Coins: © Marcel Allard / Ponopresse; Inuit artist: B. Korda / National Archives of Canada / PA-145170; Poppy: Trade-mark of the Royal Canadian Legion–used under permission; Aboriginal art: British Columbia Archives, Photo # D-02021; Canadian Coat of Arms: Department of Canadian Heritage. Reproduced with the permission of the Minister of Public Works and Government Services Canada, 2003; p. 134, Ladies playing hockey: Glenbow Archives NA-3890-14; Hockey player: Caron Rollins; p. 146, Charity run: Provincial Archives of Alberta, Photo J3019; p. 148, Citizenship ceremony: © Raffi Kirdi / Ponopresse.

© PEARSON LONGMAN • REPRODUCTION PROHIBITED

Glossary

abbreviation: a short way to write a word

abolish: to do away with, to get rid of, to make illegal

abortion: the termination or ending of a pregnancy

accommodate: to make room for; to adjust

accord: agreement

achieve: to succeed; to get

achievement: success

adapt: to adjust

addicted: feeling dependent on something and spending a great deal of time on it

agreement: in politics, a document in which countries share the same understanding about an issue

alcoholism: addiction to alcohol

allergic: suffering from a reaction to a substance

ally: partner, friend, associate

amputate: to cut off

ancestry: the cultural group from which you are descended

angst: anxiety, worries, distress

approval: permission

arranged marriage: a marriage that results when parents choose a husband or wife for their child

assimilate: to absorb, to take in

athlete: a person who is good at sports

attitude: a way of feeling or thinking about someone or something

ban: an order that forbids something from being done; to stop, to prohibit

biography: the written story of another person's life

bone-chilling: very cold

border: invisible line separating two countries or provinces

boring: not interesting

branch: a part of a large organization

brochure: a pamphlet that provides information

buffalo: a large animal that lived on the Prairies

candidate: a person who runs in an election

capital punishment: punishment by death for a crime

capture: take over

career: the general course of a person's working life; career also means chosen area of occupation

cataract: a film on the eye that can cause blindness

category: class or group

celebrate: to mark a special event

ceremony: formal celebration

chinook: dry warm wind

© PEARSON LONGMAN • REPRODUCTION PROHIBITED

© PEARSON LONGMAN • REPRODUCTION PROHIBITED

chlorofluorocarbon (CFC): a gas containing carbon, hydrogen, chlorine, and fluorine; used to refrigerate goods and as an aerosol propellant

climate: a combination of temperature, precipitation (rain or snow), wind, etc.

coach: to teach

colonies: places to live set up by Europeans outside Europe

component: part

compost: to convert organic matter to compost

conflict: disagreement or argument

connect to: join

contaminate: to make dirty

contest: competition

contribution: donation

controversial issue: an issue on which people have conflicting opinions and views

cooperation: working together

counter: to oppose

courage: bravery

crops: plants grown for food

cuisine: cooking

culture: the beliefs, values, and lifestyle of a group of people

currency: money

decade: ten years

delicacy: a rare and highly favoured food

democracy: a government that is elected by the people

deport: to send away

descendant: opposite of ancestor

desert: a dry place where little vegetation grows

desertification: becoming a desert

destroy: to ruin, to defeat

disagreement: a situation in which people or groups do not think or feel the same way about an issue

discrimination: pre-judging on the basis of sex, skin colour, religion, etc.; prejudice

disease: sickness, illness (e.g., smallpox, flu, malaria, cholera, tuberculosis)

distinct: different; unique

diversity: differences; variety

documents: legal papers

dominance: powerful influence

donate: to give

drought: continuous dry weather

economy: the system by which a country's wealth is produced and used

elect: to choose by voting

eligible: fulfilling necessary conditions

emerge: to come out

encourage: to support

endangered: threatened with extinction

ensure: to make sure

erosion: the gradual wearing away of rock or soil

escape: to get away

essential: necessary

establish: to start, to set up

exploit: to take unfair advantage of

explorer: someone who travels to places that were previously unknown

extinction: becoming extinct, no longer in existence

ferry: a boat that takes cars and/or people across water

fertilizer: chemical used to help plants grow

flock to: to gather in great numbers at a location

follow suit: to do the same thing

foothills: large hills close to mountains

force: to make someone do something

forecast: weather prediction

forestry: the industry of cutting trees and turning them into lumber and paper

frustrating: maddening; disappointing

gay: homosexual

giant: very large, huge

glorious: wonderful

gradually: slowly

greenhouse: a glass building that traps the heat from the sun to help plants grow

guide: someone who shows the way; to show the way

habitat: natural home of a plant or animal

hang: to kill someone by putting a rope around the neck (note: past tense is "hanged")

hazardous: dangerous

heritage: cultural background

hero: a champion, an inspirational person

hide: the skin of an animal

hostility: anger; animosity

identity: what a person or thing is

immersion program: a method of teaching a second language by teaching content through the new language

independent: free from authority or control; self-governing

individual: one person

industrialized nations: Europe, North America, Australia, and Japan

insect repellent: chemical used to keep insects from biting

Inuit: aboriginal people who live in the north, also called Eskimo

invade: to enter and attack

labour force: workers

landfill site: dump, place where garbage is stored

leisure time: time when a person is not working; free time

lesbian: a homosexual woman

litter: to make a place messy or dirty, to leave trash behind

log boom: a chain, cable, or line of timber used to keep logs from floating away

look forward to: to anticipate; to be excited about

majority: over 50 percent; most

marathon: a race over a very long distanc

mining: taking minerals such as gold or iron from the earth

mosaic: a collection of separate pieces that form a whole

Mountie: Royal Canadian Mounted Police (RCMP) officer

mysterious: not easy to understand

nasty: mean, cruel

national unity: one identity; shared values within a country

Native people: aboriginal people, Indians, First Nations people

network: group

neutral: neither for nor against

notify: to tell

oath: sacred promise

offender: culprit

oil refining: processing oil to make it usable

orientation: the direction of a person's thoughts, activities, or beliefs

parade: an event where people march or ride in a vehicle down the street while other people watch

parallel (of latitude): a measure of how far one is from the equator

parka: winter jacket

patient: willing to wait

patriot: love of country

pelt: animal hide; fur

penalty: a punishment such as a fine for failing to fulfill the terms of an agreement

permanent: lasting; not temporary

persistent: continuing to try despite opposition

pest: an annoying insect

polar regions: areas around the North and South poles

policy: a course of action

politician: a person whose business is politics; a person who is interested in affecting how people are governed

pollute: to cause harm to the environment

population: total number of people in a place

pothole: large hole in a road

prairie: flat, dry land

premier: the leader of a provincial government

private ownership: things belong to individuals, not to the community

proud: feeling satisfaction and pleasure about something connected to one's qualifications

racial profiling: a kind of discrimination based on racial background, ancestry, or religion

© PEARSON LONGMAN • REPRODUCTION PROHIBITED

rebellion: revolt; uprising

reception: party, gathering

reference: the name of a person who can speak on one's behalf

refrain: to stop, to keep from doing something

region: area, place

reinstate: to bring back a law

renewable: not likely to run out

representative: a person who has been chosen to act in place of another

reputation: name, status

reserve: land owned by Native people

reserved: hiding feelings

respect: appreciation, good treatment

responsibility: duty

restriction: limit

résumé: a statement of a person's work experience and education

retirement: the end of one's career

right to bear arms: the right to carry guns

right to die: the right to choose to end one's own life

rodeo: a competition in which cowboys ride wild horses, rope cattle, and perform in other events

separation: splitting up

settle: to establish a new home

settlers: people who come to live in a new land

significant: important

Sikh: a person who belongs to a religion called Sikhism

slave: a person who is owned by another person

snow sculpture: a carving made of ice and snow

sponsor: to pay for

stereotype: a standardized image or idea about a person or group of people

striking: noticeable

struggles: conflicts

subway: an underground train within a city

surf the Net: to visit many sites on the Internet

survey: to ask several questions of a number of people

survive: to continue to live, to succeed

swear allegiance: to promise loyalty

target: goal, objective

tariff: tax on imported goods or products

technology: the application of scientific knowledge

teepee: a tent made of hides and wooden poles

toques: knitted winter caps

tourism: hotels, restaurants, sightseeing tours, travel

trading post: a place where people exchange goods

tradition: beliefs; customs from the past

treason: betrayal of country; disloyalty

trend: pattern

trigger: to start

trinkets: items such as beads, bracelets, pots and pans

turban: headgear; Sikh men must wear one

ultraviolet rays: dangerous, cancer-causing rays of the sun

underemployed: having a job that does not make use of one's skills and education

unscrupulous: dishonest, corrupt

values: what people believe in

vegetarianism: the practice of not eating meat

veteran: someone who has fought in a war

vibrant: lively, exciting

violate: to show disrespect

volunteer: to give of one's time, to work for no pay

wilderness: an area of land with no development

wildlife: plants and animals in the wild

© PEARSON LONGMAN • REPRODUCTION PROHIBITED

Answer Keys

CHAPTER 1
WHAT DOES CANADA LOOK LIKE?

MULTIPLE CHOICE

1. B	3. B	5. A	7. D
2. B	4. C	6. B	

TRUE / FALSE

1. F	3. F	5. T	7. F
2. F	4. F	6. T	8. T

FILL IN THE BLANKS

1. 33	6. Toronto
2. Whitehorse	7. English, French
3. United States	8. 10, 3
4. Regina	9. Victoria
5. Newfoundland	10. Pacific, Atlantic, Arctic

MATCHING

K	Yellowknife	D	Winnipeg
G	Fredericton	A	Victoria
B	Edmonton	H	Halifax
I	Charlottetown	F	Quebec City
L	Whitehorse	J	St. John's
E	Toronto	C	Regina
M	Iqaluit		

SHORT ANSWER

1. The Atlantic, Pacific, and Arctic oceans surround Canada.
2. The Great Lakes are Lake Superior, Lake Michigan, Lake Huron, Lake Erie, and Lake Ontario.
3. The prairie provinces are Alberta, Saskatchewan, and Manitoba.
4. A chinook is a warm wind that blows over the mountains on to the prairies.
5. The territories are Northwest Territories, Yukon, and Nunavut.
6. The four Atlantic provinces are Nova Scotia, New Brunswick, Newfoundland and Labrador, and Prince Edward Island.

CHAPTER 2
CANADA'S FIRST PEOPLES

MULTIPLE CHOICE

1. C	3. B	5. A
2. D	4. B	

TRUE / FALSE

1. T	3. F.	5. T
2. F	4. T	

FILL IN THE BLANKS

1. igloos	6. hunting, fishing
2. 30 000	7. hunting (buffalo)
3. 5000	8. farming, hunting
4. 1497	9. reserves
5. 1534	

SHORT ANSWER

1. Scientists think that the Indians came to Canada across the Bering Strait.
2. The Europeans brought diseases to the Indians when they first came to Canada.
3. A reserve is land for native use only.
4. Native people value cooperation and respect for the land.
5. Today, native people face discrimination, poor education, alcoholism, and high unemployment.

CHAPTER 3
OUR ENGLISH AND FRENCH HERITAGE

MULTIPLE CHOICE

1. D	3. B	5. A
2. D	4. D	

TRUE / FALSE

1. F	3. F	5. T
2. F	4. F	

© PEARSON LONGMAN • REPRODUCTION PROHIBITED

FILL IN THE BLANKS

1. England, France
4. separate
2. Quebec
5. 1980
3. Acadians

SHORT ANSWER

1. About 80% of people living in Quebec speak French as their first language.
2. Acadia is made up of Nova Scotia and New Brunswick.
3. Most Acadians moved to Louisiana after being deported from Acadia.
4. The provincial political party that was formed in Quebec in the 1960s was the Parti Québécois.

CHAPTER 4
CONFEDERATION

MULTIPLE CHOICE

1. C	3. D	5. B	7. A
2. B	4. C	6. A	8. B

TRUE / FALSE

1. T	4. T	7. T	10. T
2. F	5. T	8. T	11. F
3. F	6. F	9. T	

FILL IN THE BLANKS

1. 1867
2. Confederation
3. Sir John A. Macdonald
4. July 1
5. November 11
6. December 25
7. January 1
8. Manitoba
9. Trudeau

MATCHING

1870 K D	1898 L
1867 E F G H	1871 A
1905 B C	1949 J
1873 I	

E	November 11	B	December 25
H	December 26	D	February 14
A	July 1	C	October 31
F	January 1	G	March 17

F	citizenship	M	recycling
M	utilities	F	currency
P	education	F	postal services
P	highways	F	immigration
M	garbage collection	F	defence
F	employment insurance	P	health care

SHORT ANSWER

1. Ontario, Quebec, Nova Scotia, and New Brunswick joined together to become Canada in 1867.
2. The national holiday of Canada is "Canada Day."

3. The British North America Act was Canada's first Constitution. It outlined the responsibilities of both the federal and provincial governments.
4. Louis Riel was a Métis who led a rebellion to stop Manitoba from joining Canada.
5. Alberta and Saskatchewan entered into Confederation in 1905.
6. The three levels of government in Canada are federal, provincial, and municipal.
7. Federal responsibilities include citizenship, defence, post office, unemployment insurance, foreign policy, currency, Canada Pension, RCMP, and immigration.
8. Provincial responsibilities include health care, education, licenses, and highways.
9. Municipal responsibilities include garbage collection, utilities, recycling, water, fire protection, streets, and city police.

CHAPTER 5
TYING THE NATION TOGETHER

MULTIPLE CHOICE

1. B	3. C	5. A
2. B	4. C	

TRUE / FALSE

1. F	3. F	5. F
2. T	4. T	6. T

MATCHING

G	1991	B	1914
E	1939	D	1812
F	1756	A	1950
C	1869		

SHORT ANSWER

1. The government bought land to enlarge the size of the country and to build the Canadian Pacific Railway.
2. John A. Macdonald wanted Canada to stretch from sea to sea.
3. John A. Macdonald wanted to build the Canadian Pacific Railway to unite the country.
4. The Canadian Shield and the Rocky Mountains made it difficult and dangerous to build the Canadian Pacific Railway.
5. The Canadian Pacific Railway was used for travel and transportation of goods (e.g., wheat).
6. Many people moved to Canada from the United States because they were loyal to the King of England.
7. The border between Canada and the United States was established at the end of the war in 1812.
8. Canadians won the Battle of Vimy Ridge. Canada emerged as a growing power in the world.

© PEARSON LONGMAN • REPRODUCTION PROHIBITED

CHAPTER 6
CANADA TODAY: A DIVERSE SOCIETY

MULTIPLE CHOICE
1. B   3. D   5. C
2. B   4. D

TRUE / FALSE
1. T   3. F   5. F
2. T   4. T   6. T

FILL IN THE BLANKS
1. 1988   3. first
2. mosaic   4. Non-Europeans

SHORT ANSWER
1. The federal government wanted to settle the west.
2. Points are awarded for occupation, language ability, education, work experience, and financial status.
3. The greatest immigration occurred prior to World War I: 1905-1913.
4. People came to Canada in the late 1800s because they wanted freedom. In addition, many poor people could afford to buy land.

CHAPTER 7
WHAT DO CANADIANS DO?

TRUE / FALSE
1. T   3. T   5. T   7. F
2. F   4. T   6. F   8. F

SHORT ANSWER
1. Natural resources in British Columbia are forests, fish, minerals, and fruit.
2. Industries in Prince Edward Island are potato farming and tourism.
3. The main industries in Quebec are manufacturing, hydroelectricity, mining, dairy farming, and tourism.
4. The main industries in Manitoba are farming and hydroelectricity.
5. The main industries in Ontario are manufacturing, mining, fruit, and tourism.
6. The main industries in New Brunswick are forestry and food processing.
7. One of the most important changes in the workplace in Canada is that women have joined the work force.
8. Canadians enjoy swimming, fishing, gardening, bicycling, walking, camping, and hiking during the summer.
9. Canadians enjoy skiing, skidooing, skating, hockey, reading, and watching TV during the winter.
10. Christianity has the biggest following in Canada.

CHAPTER 8
CANADA IN A GLOBAL WORLD

MULTIPLE CHOICE
1. C   2. D   3. A   4. A

SHORT ANSWER
1. Release of gases (such as carbon dioxide, methane, and CFCs) into the atmosphere
2. Plants, fish, and animals die; damages buildings, damages human health
3. Soil erosion, desertification, the greenhouse effect
4. Rise in skin cancer, destruction of crops
5. Reduce, reuse, recycle
6. Greater access to information, improved health care, access to consumer goods
7. Homogenization of cultures, rich corporations get richer while poor people get poorer

CHAPTER 9
HOW IS CANADA GOVERNED?

MULTIPLE CHOICE
1. C   4. A   7. D   10. A
2. B   5. B   8. C   11. B
3. A   6. D   9. C

TRUE / FALSE
1. F   3. F   5. F   7. T   9. T
2. T   4. F   6. F   8. F   10. F

FILL IN THE BLANKS
1. Ask your teacher   7. Legislative Assembly (legislature)
2. three   8. Premier
3. Senate   9. Mayor, Councillors
4. Government   10. Bill
5. Official Opposition 11. Royal assent
6. Prime Minister

MATCHING
C The Queen's representative in the Provincial government
F Appointed by the Prime Minister
G The leader of the party with the most MLAs elected
A The leader of the party with the most MPs elected
D A person who is elected to the provincial government
B The Queen's representative in the Federal government
E The party with the second most MPs elected
H A person who is elected to the federal government

© PEARSON LONGMAN • REPRODUCTION PROHIBITED

SHORT ANSWER

1. The Governor General represents the Queen in the federal government.
2. Members of Parliament are elected people in the House of Commons.
3. Members of Parliament are elected by the people.
4. Senators are appointed by the Prime Minister.
5. The Prime Minister is the leader of the party that has the most elected MPs.
6. Cabinet Ministers give advice and help in certain areas of the government, for example, Finance and Defence.
7. The Lieutenant Governor represents the Queen in the provincial government.
8. The Premier is the leader of the party who has the most elected MLAs.
9. A bill is a piece of legislation or a suggestion for a law that is written down.
10. Royal assent occurs when the Governor General signs a bill.
11. If a person is accused of a crime, he/she must be treated fairly and all legal rights must be respected.
12. The government, the police, and the courts.

CHAPTER 10
ELECTIONS

MULTIPLE CHOICE

1. A	3. C	5. A	7. B	9. C
2. A	4. C	6. A	8. A	

TRUE / FALSE

1. F	3. T	5. F	7. T
2. F	4. F	6. F	

FILL IN THE BLANKS

1. five
2. three
3. polling station
4. ballot
5. 8 p.m.
6. Prime Minister
7. independent
8. scrutineer

ORDERING

2 Eligible voters receive a voter information card in the mail.
5 The voter goes to a polling booth and votes.
7 The votes are counted.
6 The ballot is put into a locked box.
8 The winners of the election are announced.
3 Voters go the polling station to vote.
4 The voter's name is crossed off the list and the voter is given a ballot.
1 The Prime Minister calls an election.

SHORT ANSWER

1. A representative democracy means that the people elect representatives to make decisions for them.
2. A voters' list is a list of people eligible to vote in an election.
3. A riding or a constituency is a geographical section or area of the country. People who live in the riding choose a candidate to represent them.
4. Canadian voters find out about the ideas of the different parties by listening to the radio, watching the television, going to community meetings, talking to friends, reading the newspaper, and reading brochures delivered to them.
5. The role of the poll clerk is to make sure each person who comes to vote is eligible. They also ensure that a person only votes once.
6. A secret ballot means that no one sees who a person votes for.
7. Scrutineers ensure that voting is done properly.
8. A person becomes a Member of Parliament by being elected.
9. The federal parties in Canada include the Liberal Party, the Conservative Party, the Green Party, the New Democratic Party, and the Bloc Québécois.

CHAPTER 11
WHO ARE THESE CANADIANS?

MATCHING

H A famous Canadian hockey player
I Former PM of Canada
G The first Canadian astronaut in space
A A young Canadian who wanted to raise money for cancer research
E A Métis author
B A writer who fought for women's rights in Canada
C One of two scientists who helped discover insulin
D The first woman Governor General
F A famous Canadian surgeon

SHORT ANSWER

1. Terry Fox was a young man who wanted to run across Canada to raise money for cancer research.
2. The "Terry Fox Run" is an annual run that takes place each September to raise money for cancer research.
3. Emily Murphy was an advocate of women's rights in Canada. Because of her efforts, women were declared persons under the law.

© PEARSON LONGMAN • REPRODUCTION PROHIBITED

4. Dr. Norman Bethune was famous because he helped both the Spanish and the Chinese during their civil wars.

5. Dr. Frederick Banting and Dr. Charles Best discovered insulin used to fight diabetes.

6. The Victoria Cross is a military honour and is awarded for bravery and courage in the face of an enemy.

CHAPTER 12
WHAT IS TYPICALLY CANADIAN?

TRUE / FALSE

1. F   3. T   5. F   7. T   9. T
2. T   4. T   6. F   8. T

FILL IN THE BLANKS

1. French, English   4. Maple leaf
2. Quebec   5. Hockey
3. Poppy

MATCHING

H "a mari usque ad mare"
E Canada's national police force
A symbol on the Canadian flag
B symbol on the nickel
G nickname for the Canadian dollar
C symbol on the Quebec flag
D symbol of Remembrance Day
F located in Ottawa

SHORT ANSWER

1. A National park is an area of land owned and administered by the federal government. National parks are designed to preserve the wilderness for Canadians to enjoy.

2. Canada is a bilingual country because there are two official languages: French and English. All federal services can be accessed in either French or English.

3. Canada is a multicultural country because its citizens are descendants from many different countries and cultures.

4. Canadians call their dollar coin a loonie because there is a picture of a loon on many of the dollar coins.

5. A goal of multiculturalism is to treat all Canadians as different but equal.

CHAPTER 13
BECOMING A CANADIAN

MULTIPLE CHOICE

1. A   3. D   5. D
2. C   4. B   6. C

TRUE / FALSE

1. F   3. T   5. T   7. T
2. F   4. F   6. F

FILL IN THE BLANKS

1. freedom of religion   4. The Charter of Rights and Freedoms
2. more   5. right
3. responsibilities   6. volunteerism

SHORT ANSWER

1. The freedoms Canadians enjoy are the freedom of religion, the freedom of thought, belief, opinion and expression, and the freedom of peaceful assembly.

2. The rights Canadians enjoy are the right to vote in elections, the right to live and work anywhere in Canada, the right to run in an election, the right to be treated equally, and various legal rights.

3. The responsibilities of Canadians are the responsibility to vote in elections, the responsibility to be loyal to Canada, responsibility to learn and obey the laws of the country, the responsibility to refrain from discrimination against others, the responsibility to participate in the community and to care for Canada's heritage.

4. Freedom of the press means that the news media can print any stories that they know to be true. The government cannot stop them from printing a story.

© PEARSON LONGMAN • REPRODUCTION PROHIBITED

Pearson Education ESL Canadian Titles and Authors

Canadian Stories by Eleanor Adamowski

The Longman Picture Dictionary, Canadian ed., by Julie Ashworth & John Clark

Reading for the Write Reasons: English Reading and Writing for Advanced ESL Students by Donna Aziz-Canuel, Lynne Gaetz & Richard Pawsey

Amazing! Canadian Newspaper Stories by Susan Bates

Amazing! News Interviews & Conversations by Susan Bates

Amazing 2! Canadian Newspaper Stories by Susan Bates

Amazing 2! News Interviews & Conversations by Susan Bates

Canadian Concepts, 2nd ed., Books 1-6 by Lynda Berish & Sandra Thibaudeau

English Fast Forward 1, 2nd ed., by Lynda Berish & Sandra Thibaudeau

English Fast Forward 2, 2nd ed., by Lynda Berish & Sandra Thibaudeau

English Fast Forward 3, 2nd ed., by Lynda Berish & Sandra Thibaudeau

Grammar Connections, Books 1, 2 & 3, by Lynda Berish & Sandra Thibaudeau

On Target by Keith L. Boeckner & Joan Polfuss Boeckner

On Target Too by Keith L. Boeckner & Joan Polfuss Boeckner

Target Practice by Keith L. Boeckner & Joan Polfuss Boeckner

Classics Canada: Authentic Readings for ESL Students, Books 1-4, by Patricia Brock & Brian John Busby

Coming to Canada: Authentic Reading for ESL Students by Patricia Brock & Brian John Busby

Contemporary Canada: Authentic Readings for ESL Students by Patricia Brock & Brian John Busby

Being Canadian, 2nd ed., by Judy Cameron & Tracey M. Derwing

A Canadian Conversation Book: English in Everyday Life, 2nd ed., Book 1, by Tina Kasloff Carver, Sandra Douglas Fotinos & Clarice Cooper

Focus 2: Academic Listening and Speaking Skills by Ranka Curcin, Mary Koumoulas, & Sonia Fiorucci-Nicholls

Focus 2: Academic Reading Skills by Ranka Curcin, Mary Koumoulas, & Sonia Fiorucci-Nicholls

Focus 2: Academic Writing Skills by Ranka Curcin, Mary Koumoulas, & Sonia Fiorucci-Nicholls

Technically Speaking…: Writing, Reading and Listening, English at Work by Susan Quirk Drolet & Ann Farrell Séguin

Take Charge: Using Everyday Canadian English by Lucia Pietrusiak Engkent

Take Part: Speaking Canadian English, 2nd ed., by Lucia Pietrusiak Engkent & Karen P. Bardy

Writing for Success: Preparing for Business, Technology, Trades and Career Programs by Dale Fitzpatrick & Kathleen Center Vance

All Right! A Guide to Correct English by Paul Fournier

Blueprints: A Guide to Correct Writing by Paul Fournier

English on Demand, 2nd ed., by Paul Fournier

English on Line, 2nd ed., by Paul Fournier

English on Purpose, 2nd ed., by Paul Fournier

This Side Up by Paul Fournier

This Way Out by Paul Fournier

Before Brass Tacks: Basic Grammar by Lynne Gaetz

Before Brass Tacks: Basic Skills in English by Lynne Gaetz

Brass Ring 1: Basic English for Career-Related Communication by Lynne Gaetz

Brass Ring 1: Basic Grammar Review by Lynne Gaetz

Brass Ring 2: English for Career-Related Communication by Lynne Gaetz

Brass Ring 2: Grammar Review by Lynne Gaetz

Brass Tacks Grammar by Lynne Gaetz

Brass Tacks: Integrated Skills in English by Lynne Gaetz

Open Book English Skills by Lynne Gaetz

Open Book Grammar by Lynne Gaetz

Open Road English Skills by Lynne Gaetz

Open Road Grammar by Lynne Gaetz

Open Window English Skills by Lynne Gaetz

Open Window Grammar by Lynne Gaetz

Bridge to Fluency by Elizabeth Gatbonton

Links: ESL Writing and Editing by Carolyn Greene & Claudia Rock

A Beginning Look at Canada, 3rd ed., by Anne-Marie Kaskens

Writing for Results: Academic and Professional Writing Tasks by H. M. McGarell & P. Brillinger

Reading Matters: A Selection of Canadian Writing by Jane Merivale

Word-by-Word Beginning Workbook, Canadian ed. by Steven Molinsky & Bill Bliss

Word-by-Word Intermediate Workbook, Canadian ed. by Steven Molinsky & Bill Bliss

Word-by-Word Picture Dictionary, Canadian ed. by Steven Molinsky & Bill Bliss

Getting it Together, Books 1 & 2, by Véra Téophil Naber

A Grammar Manual, Volumes A & B, by Véra Téophil Naber & Savitsa Sévigny

Style and Substance: A Multimedia Approach to Literature and Composition by Claudia Rock & Suneeti Phadke

Read on Canada by Paul Sharples & Judith Clark

Advanced Half-Hour Helper: Puzzles and Activities for ESL Students by Joan Roberta White

Half-Hour Helper: Puzzles and Activities for ESL Students by Joan Roberta White

Making the Grade: An Interactive Course in English for Academic Purposes by David Wood

© PEARSON LONGMAN • REPRODUCTION PROHIBITED